All-Time Favorite Parking Lot Fingerstyle Guitar Solos

by Mike McAdoo

I0803029

Features 19 easy to intermediate fingerstyle guitar arrangements.
Familiar folk, old-time and gospel favorites.
Every tune is set in a guitar-friendly key. Written in standard notation and tablature.
Includes downloadable audio for ease of learning.

Online Audio

To access the online audio recording go to:
WWW.MELBAY.COM/31091MEB

The OM2H-T Traditional guitar images on the cover are courtesy of Collings Guitars.

MEL BAY

WWW.MELBAY.COM

Preface

In these 19 easy to intermediate fingerstyle guitar arrangements of familiar folk and gospel favorites, I've tried to preserve the original melodies of the tunes while coming up with something that lies well on the fretboard. If it swings a little, that's fine too.

You may notice that some of my bass lines reflect the influence of Chet Atkins' signature alternating bass figures. These bass lines can be played with or without a thumb pick, either short and slightly muted with the heel and wrist of the picking hand on the low strings, or full voiced without the muted effect. Muting is easier, however, if you play with a thumb pick because the pick leaves your other fingers free to pluck at a better angle.

I've included online audio recordings as a guide to novice notation and tab readers, and as evidence that my arrangements can be played by human beings. I hope you find them musically rewarding and fun to play. It would be a great compliment if my arrangements inspired you to write arrangements of your own.

Contents

Title	Page	Audio
Aura Lee	4	1
Amazing Grace	6	2
Do Lord	7	3
Banks of the Ohio	8	4
Cotton-Eyed Joe	10	5
Greensleeves	11	6
Buffalo Gals	14	7
Nine Pound Hammer	16	8
In the Garden	18	9
Red Wing	20	10
Roll in My Sweet Baby's Arms	22	11
The Crawdad Song	23	12
Sweet By and By	24	13
The Old Rugged Cross	26	14
Wayfarin' Stranger	28	15
When the Roll Is Called Up Yonder	30	16
Just a Closer Walk with Thee	32	17
Just as I Am	33	18
Wildwood Flower	34	19

Aura Lee

Intro

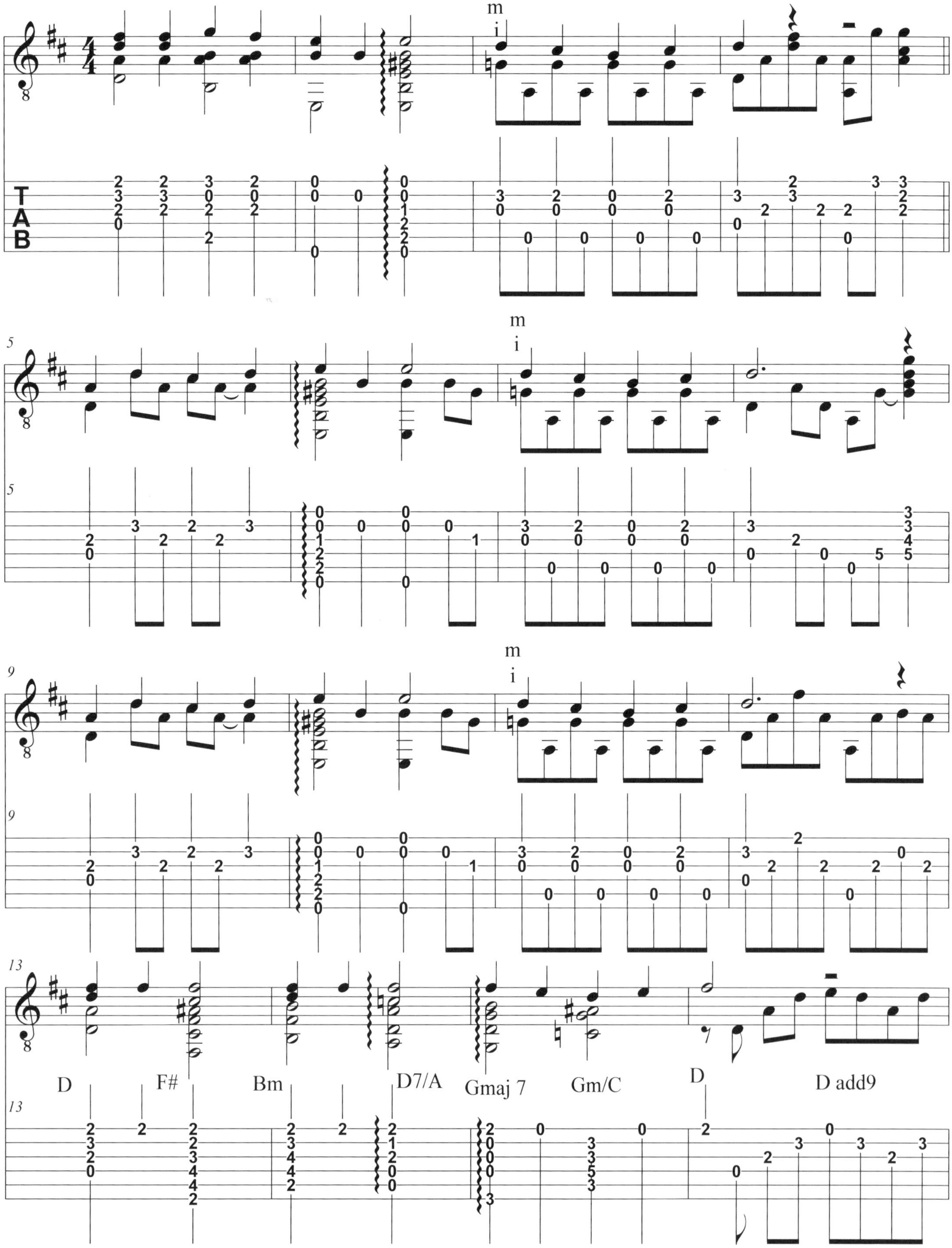

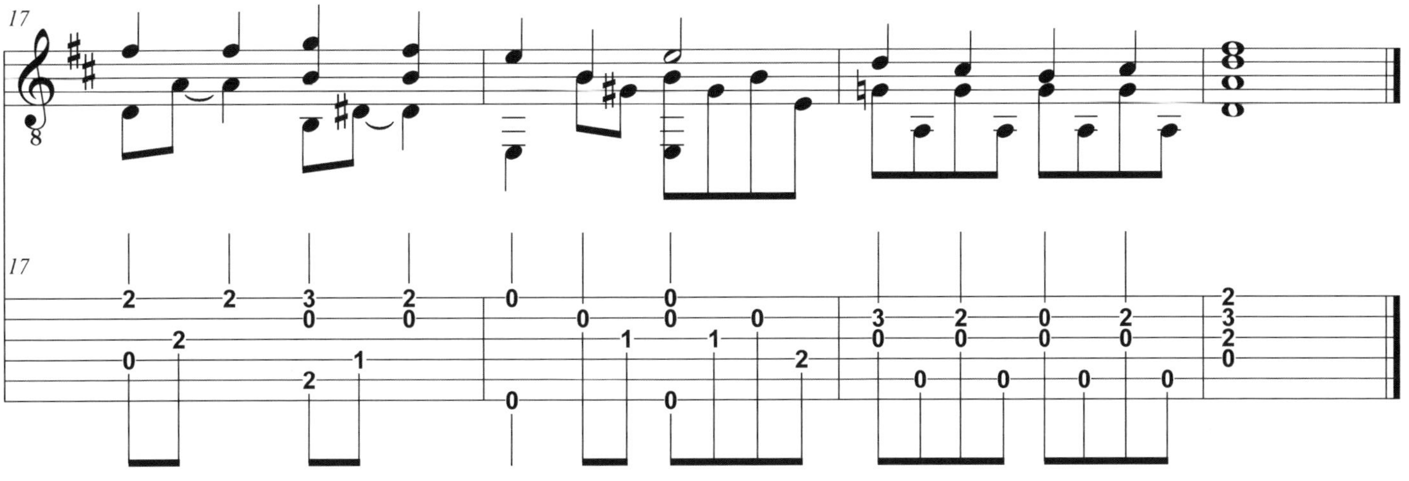

Amazing Grace

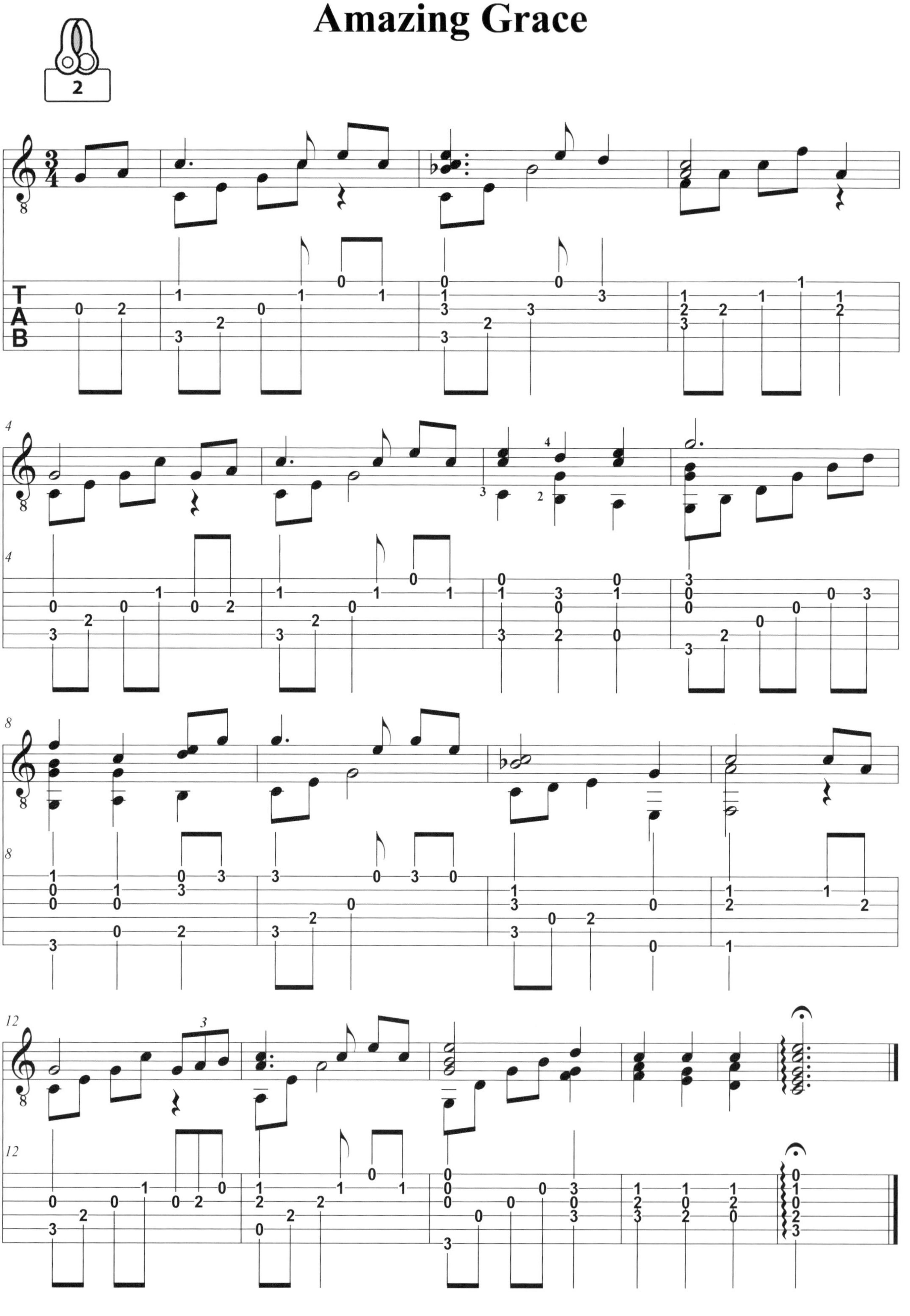

Do Lord

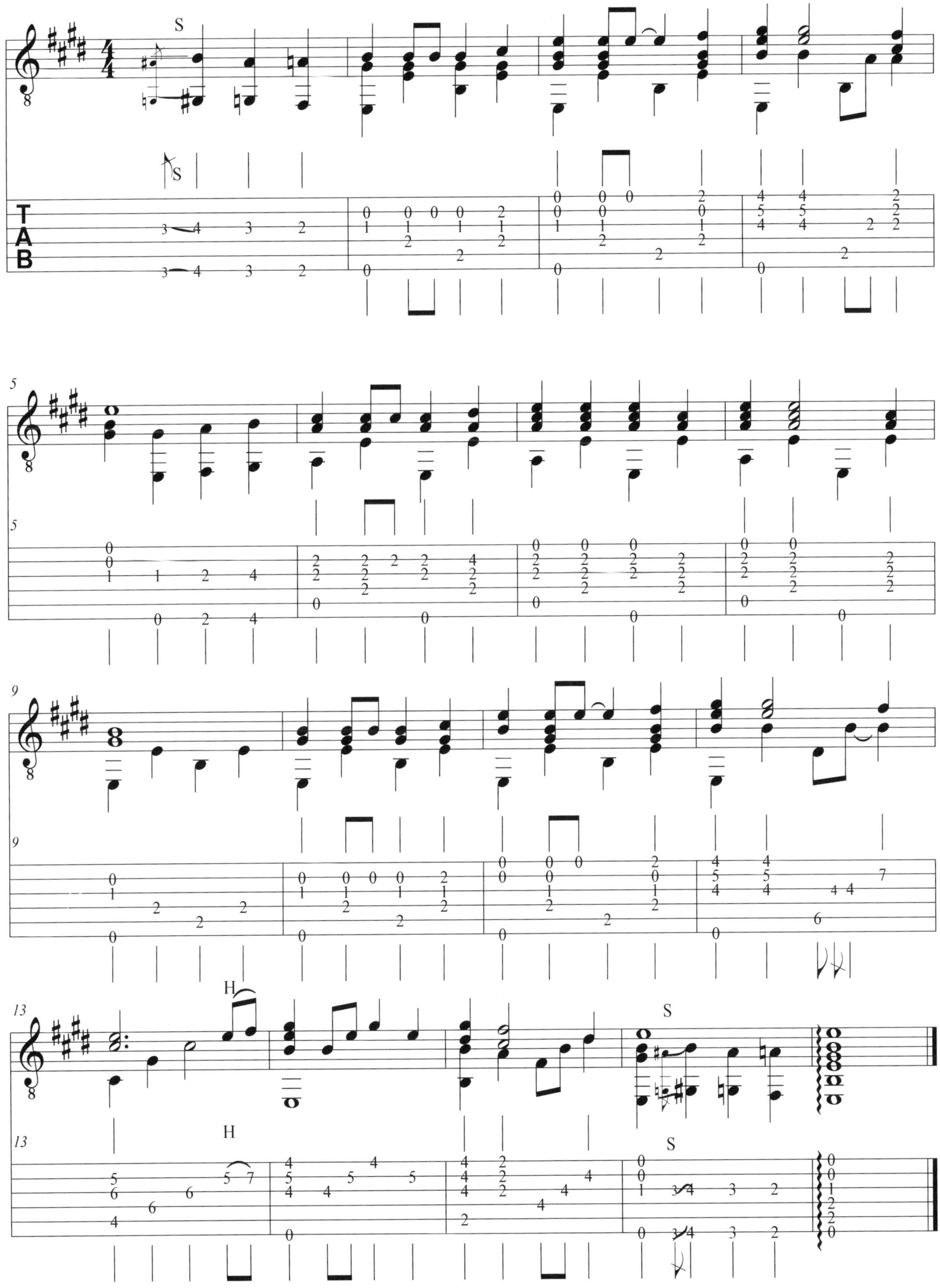

Banks of the Ohio

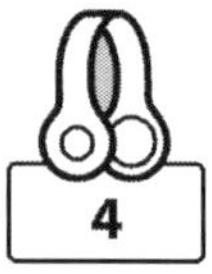

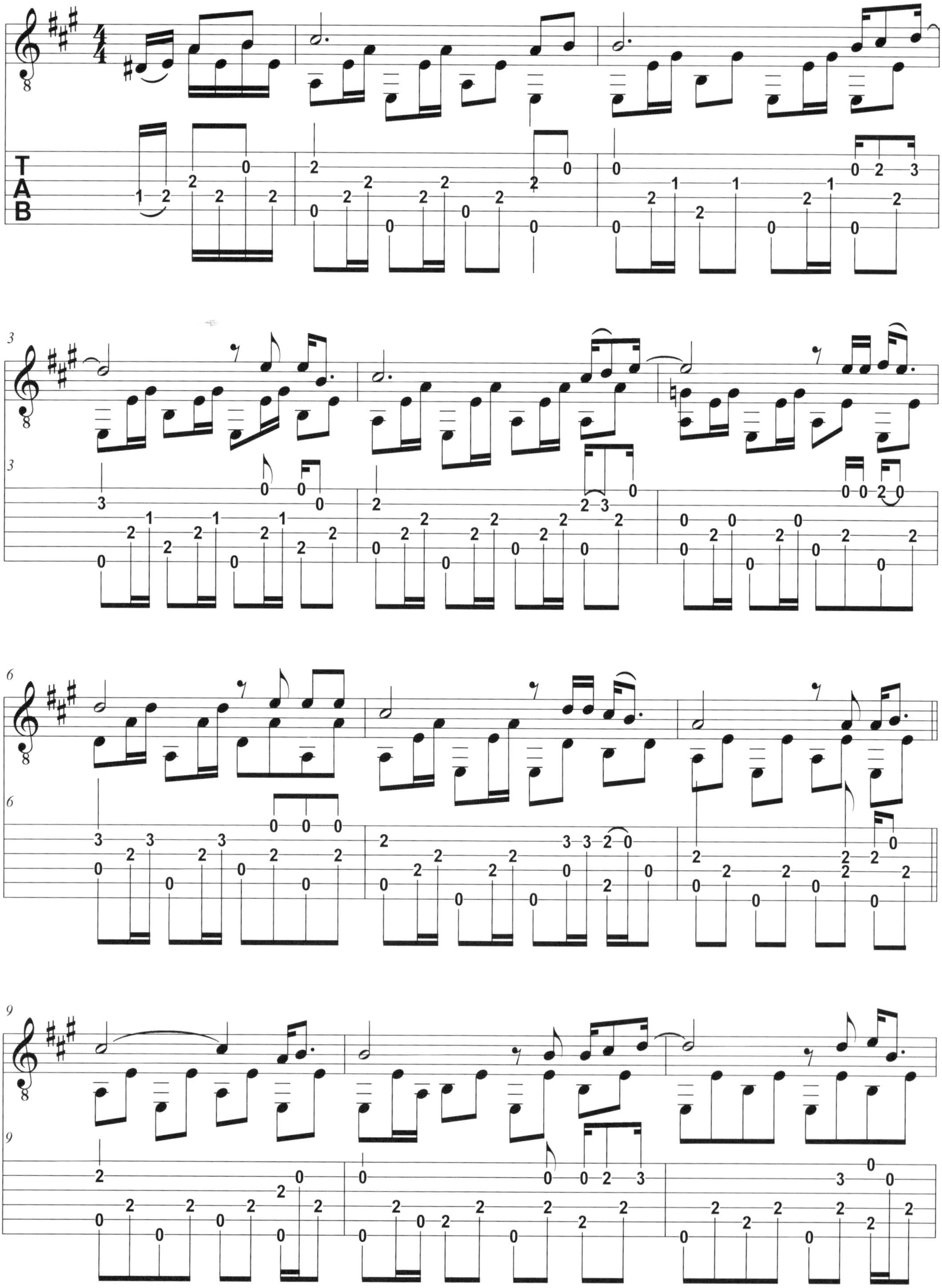

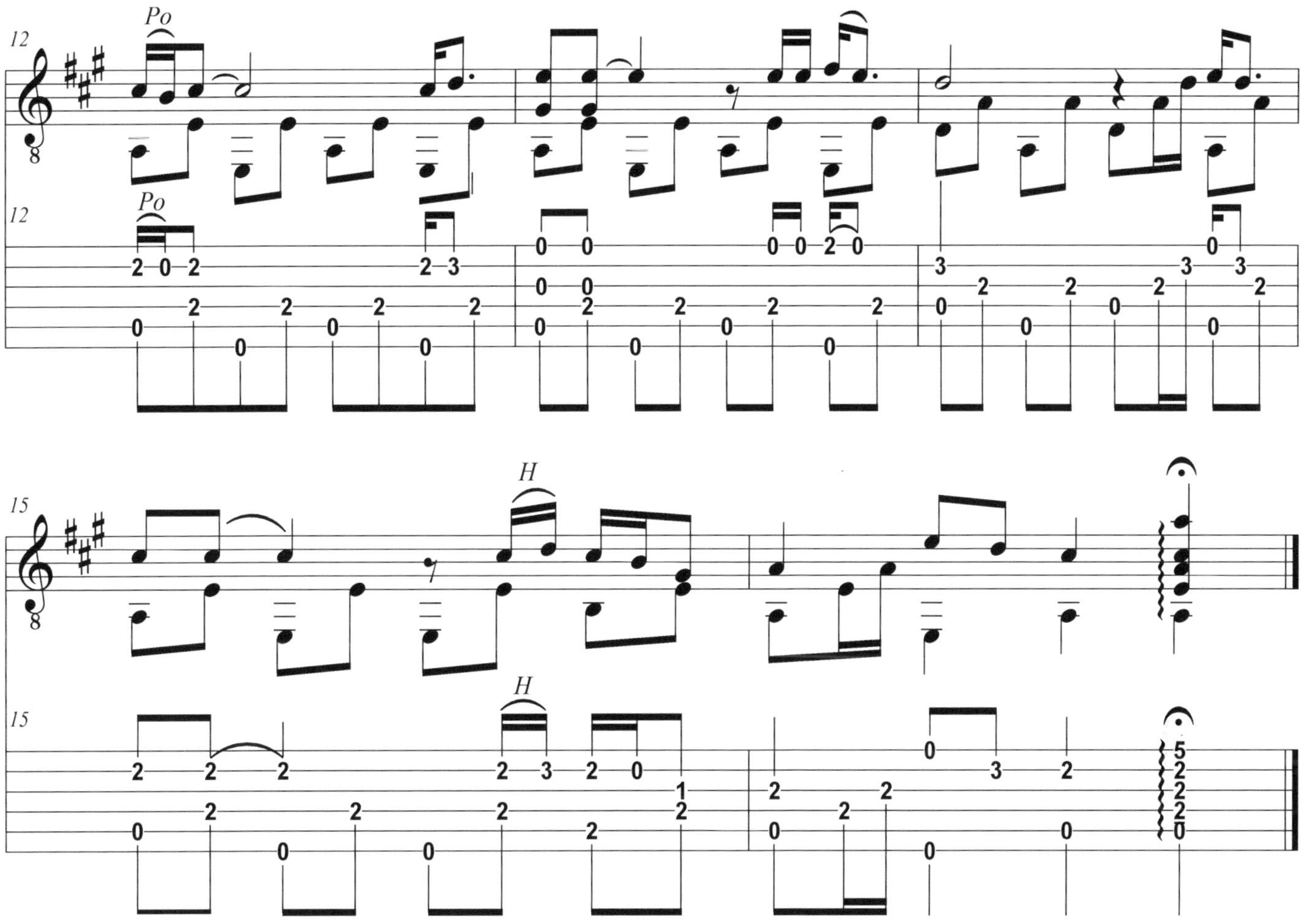
Po
Po
H
H

Cotton-Eyed Joe

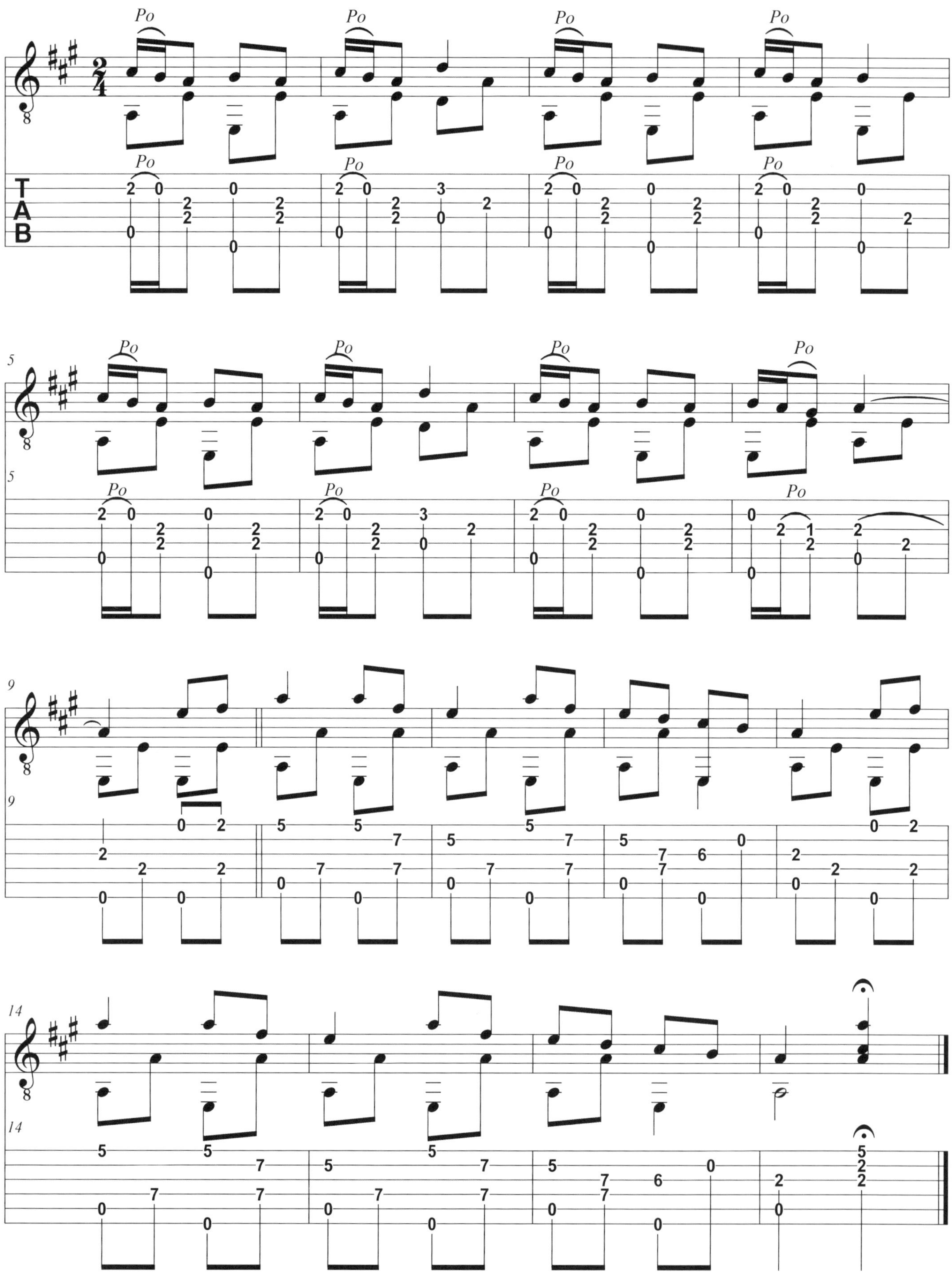

Greensleeves

6

Intro:

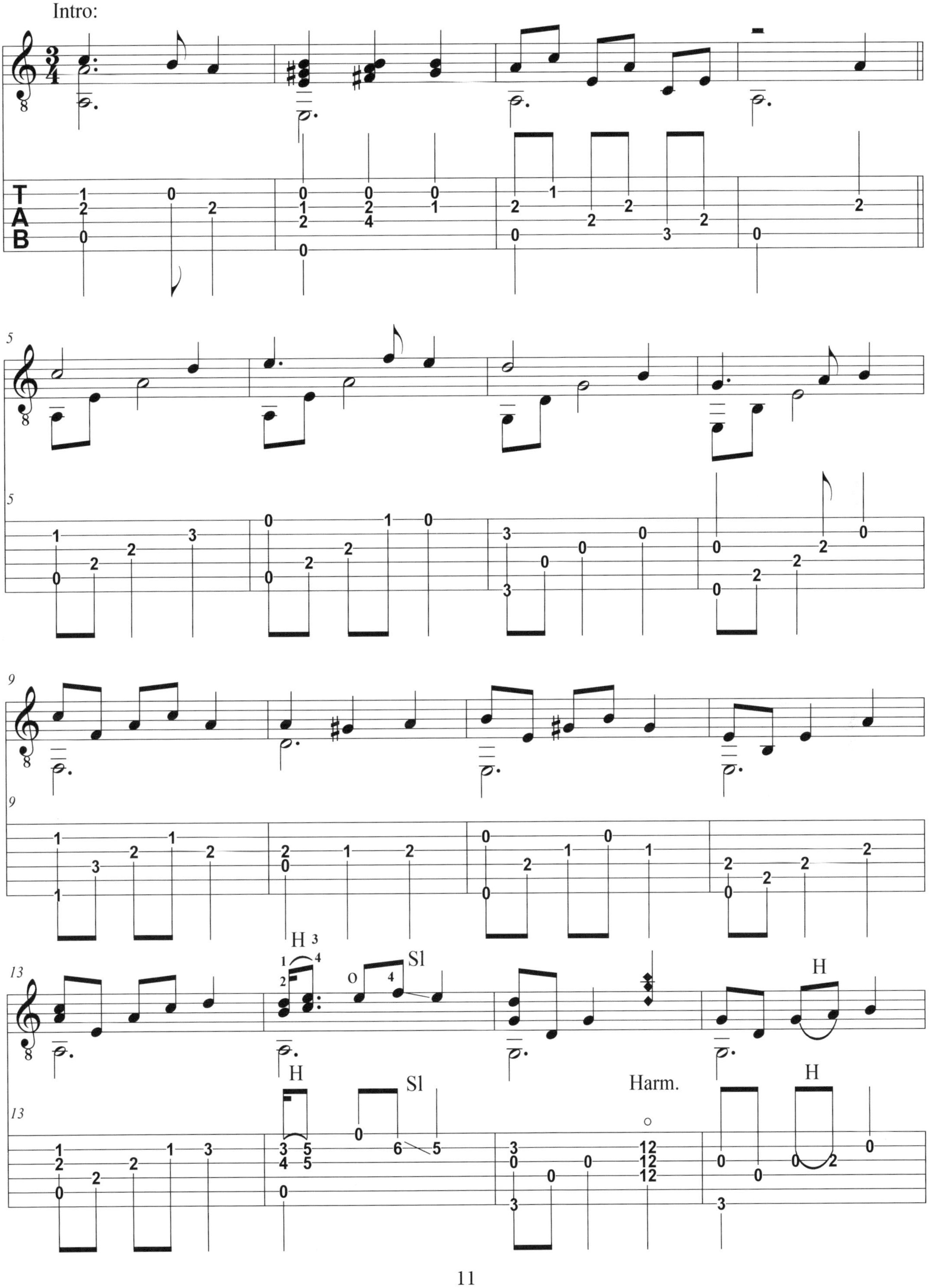

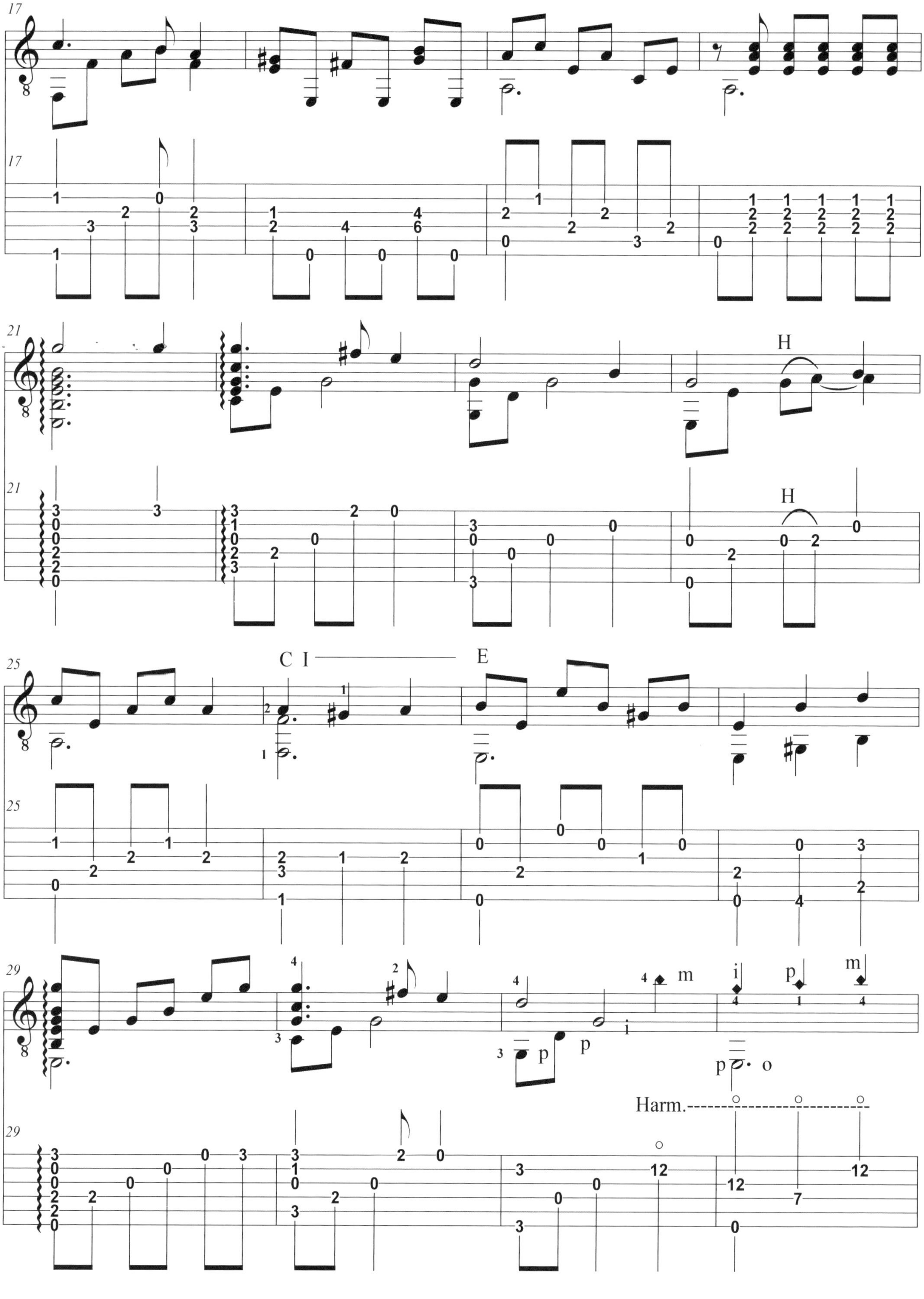

H
C I
E
Harm.

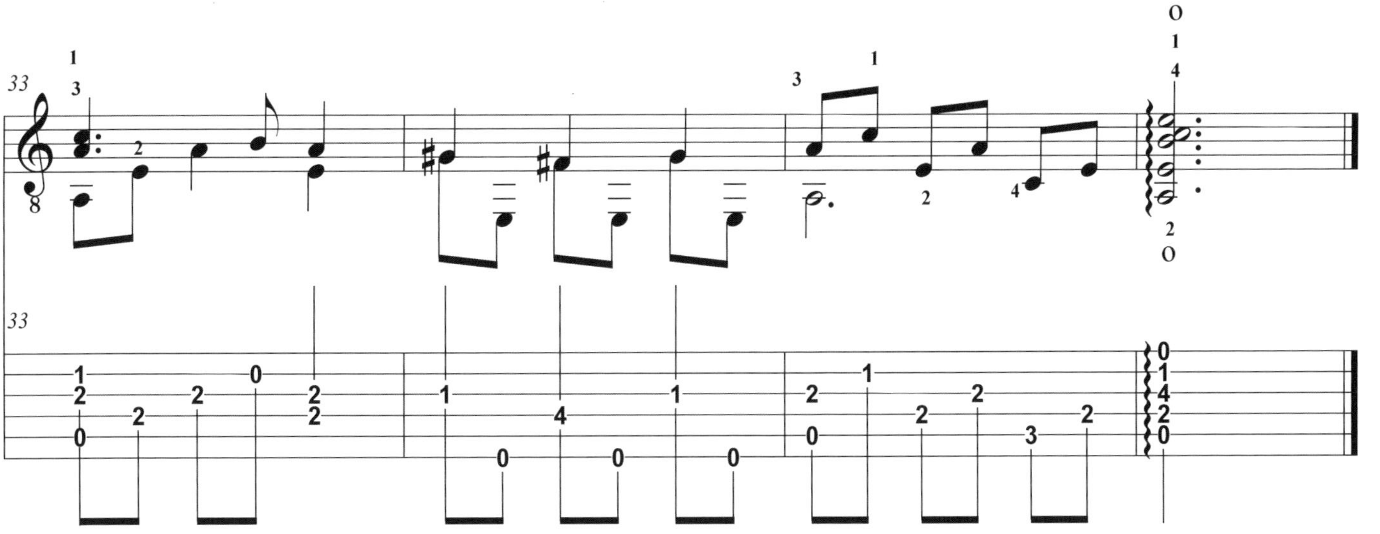

Buffalo Gals

7

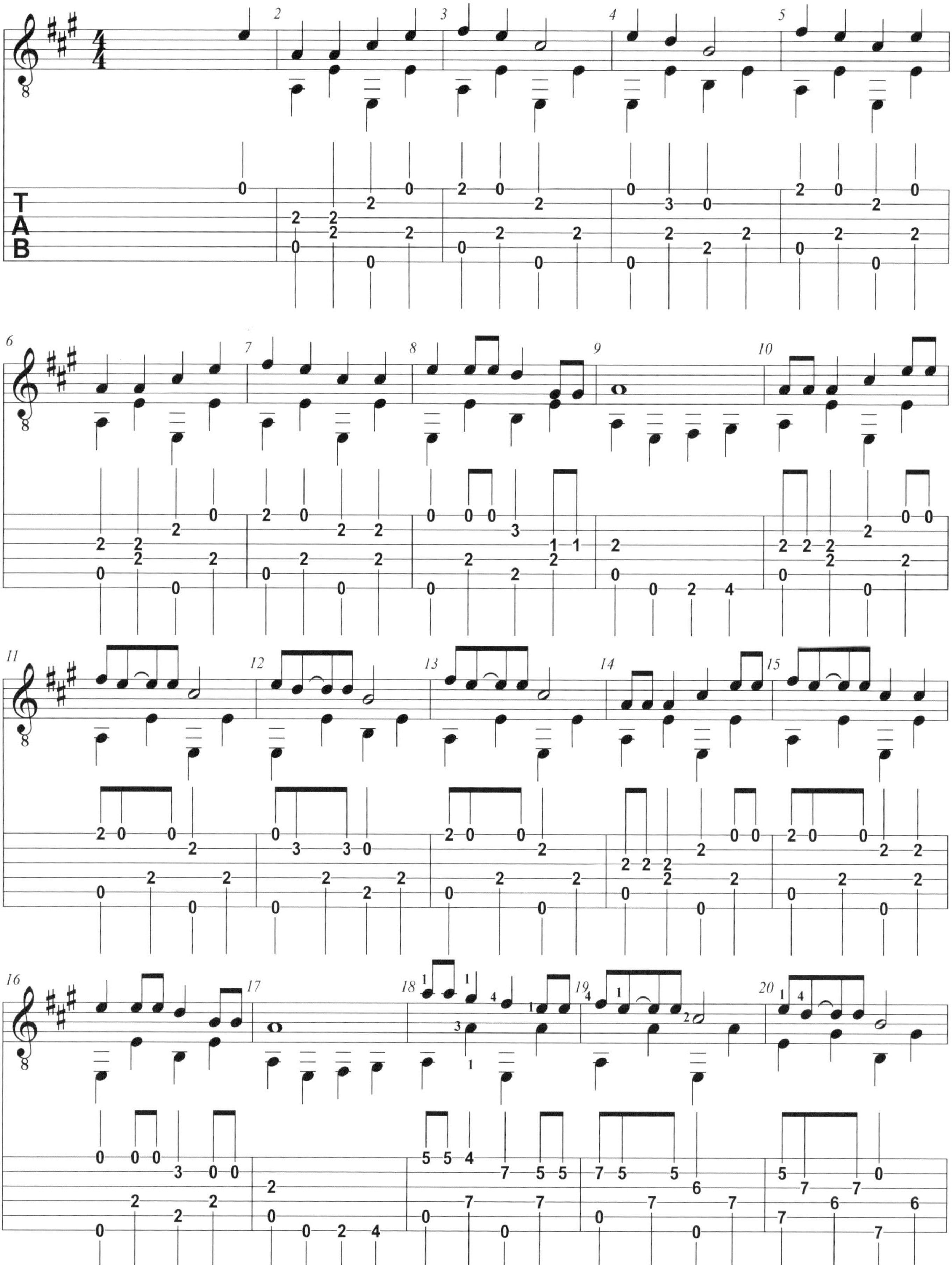

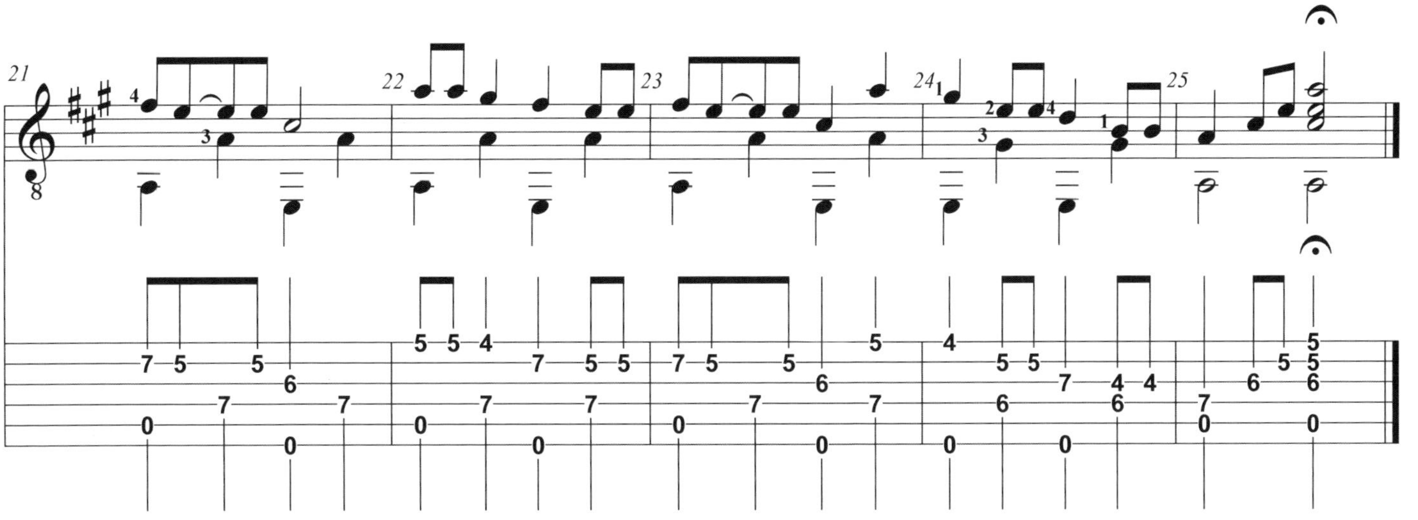

Nine Pound Hammer

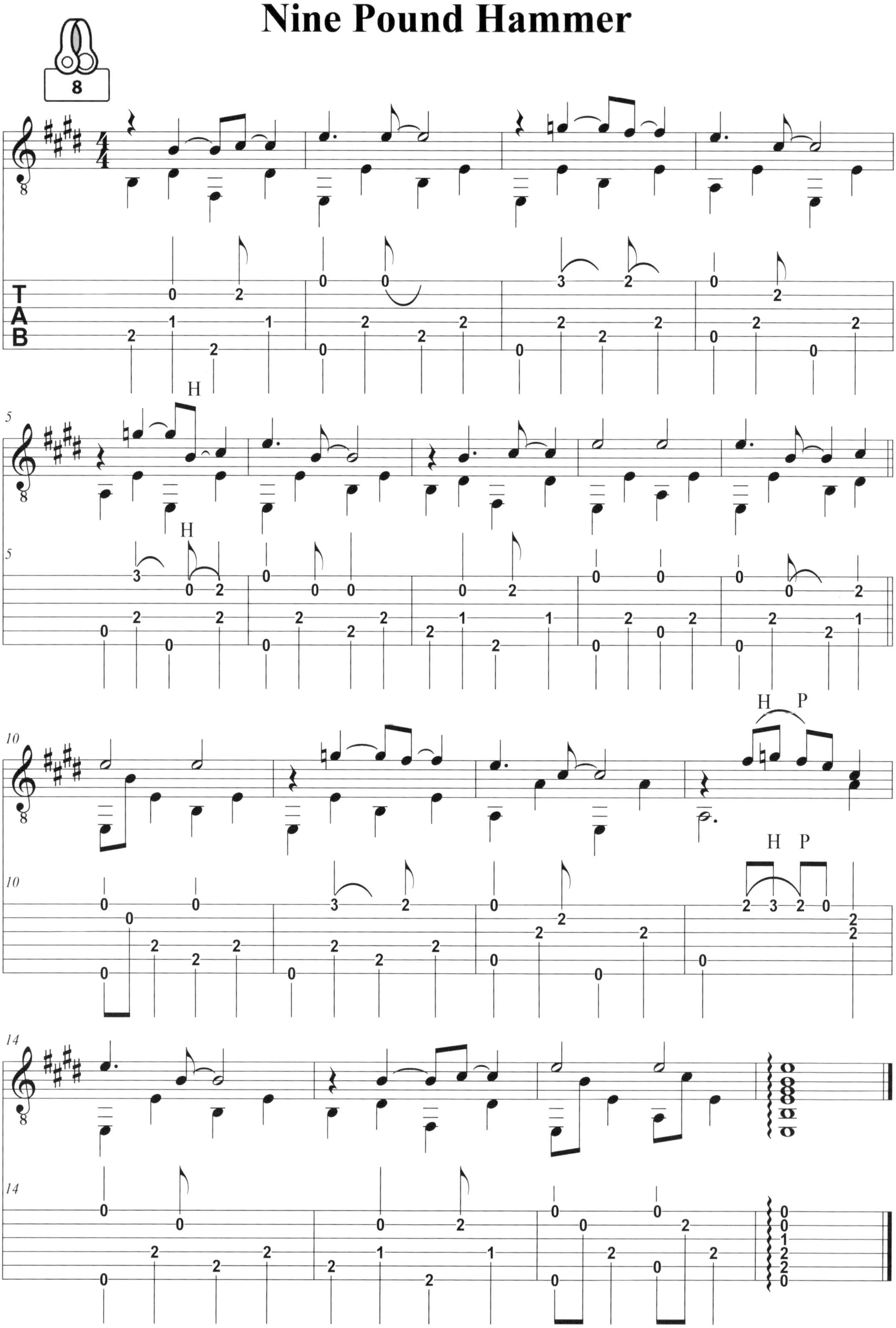

This page has been left blank to avoid an awkward page turn.

In the Garden

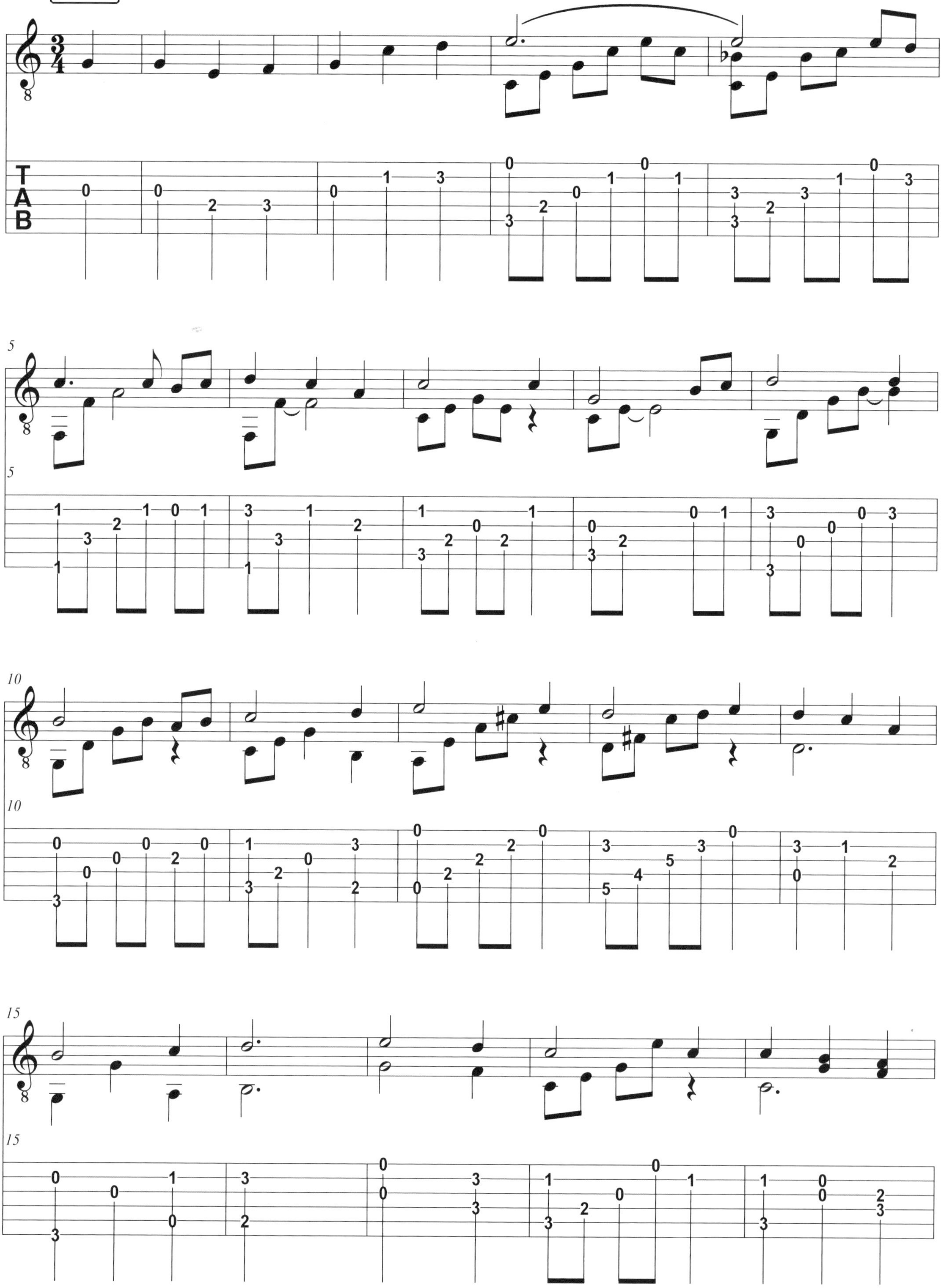

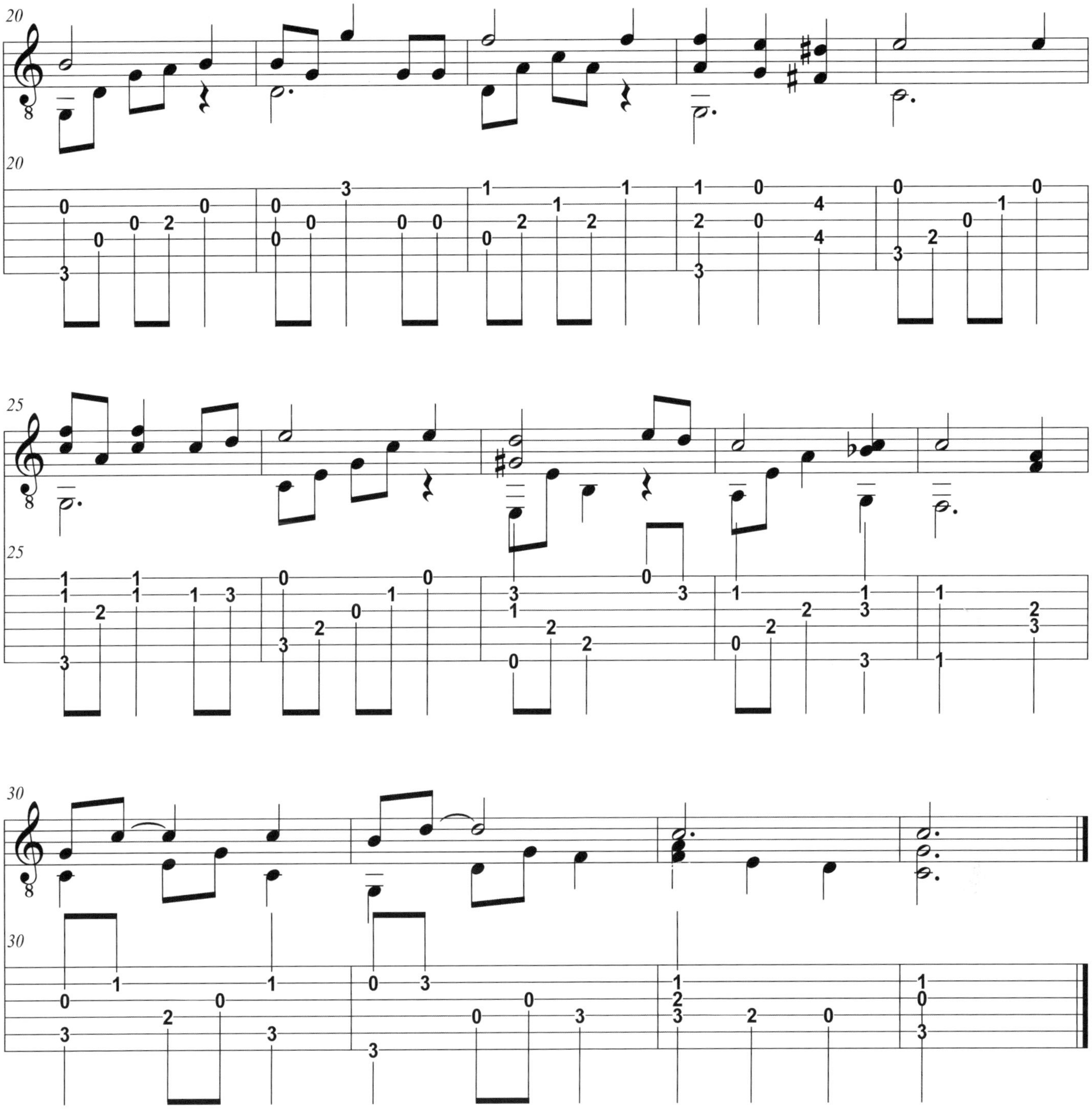

10

Red Wing

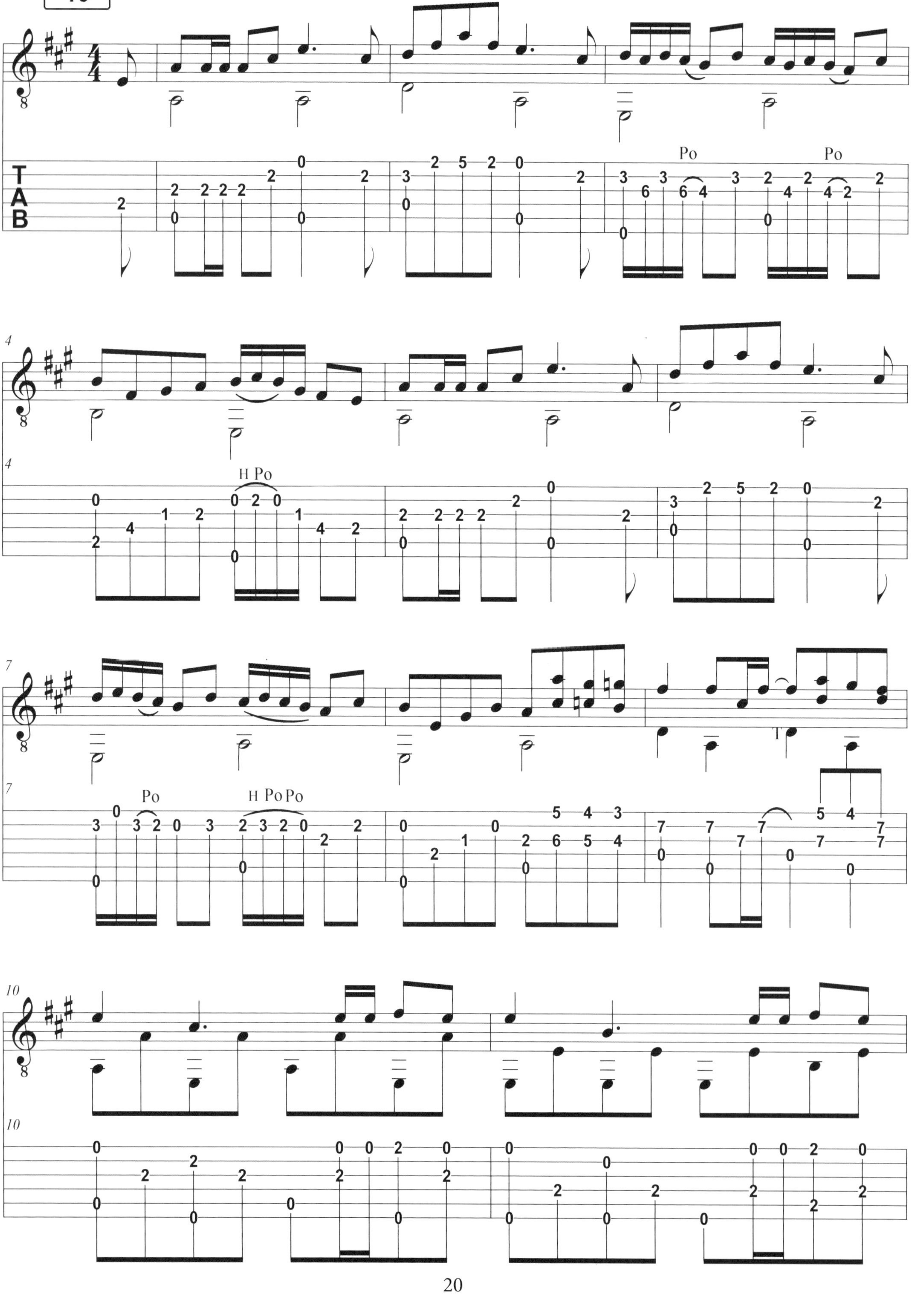

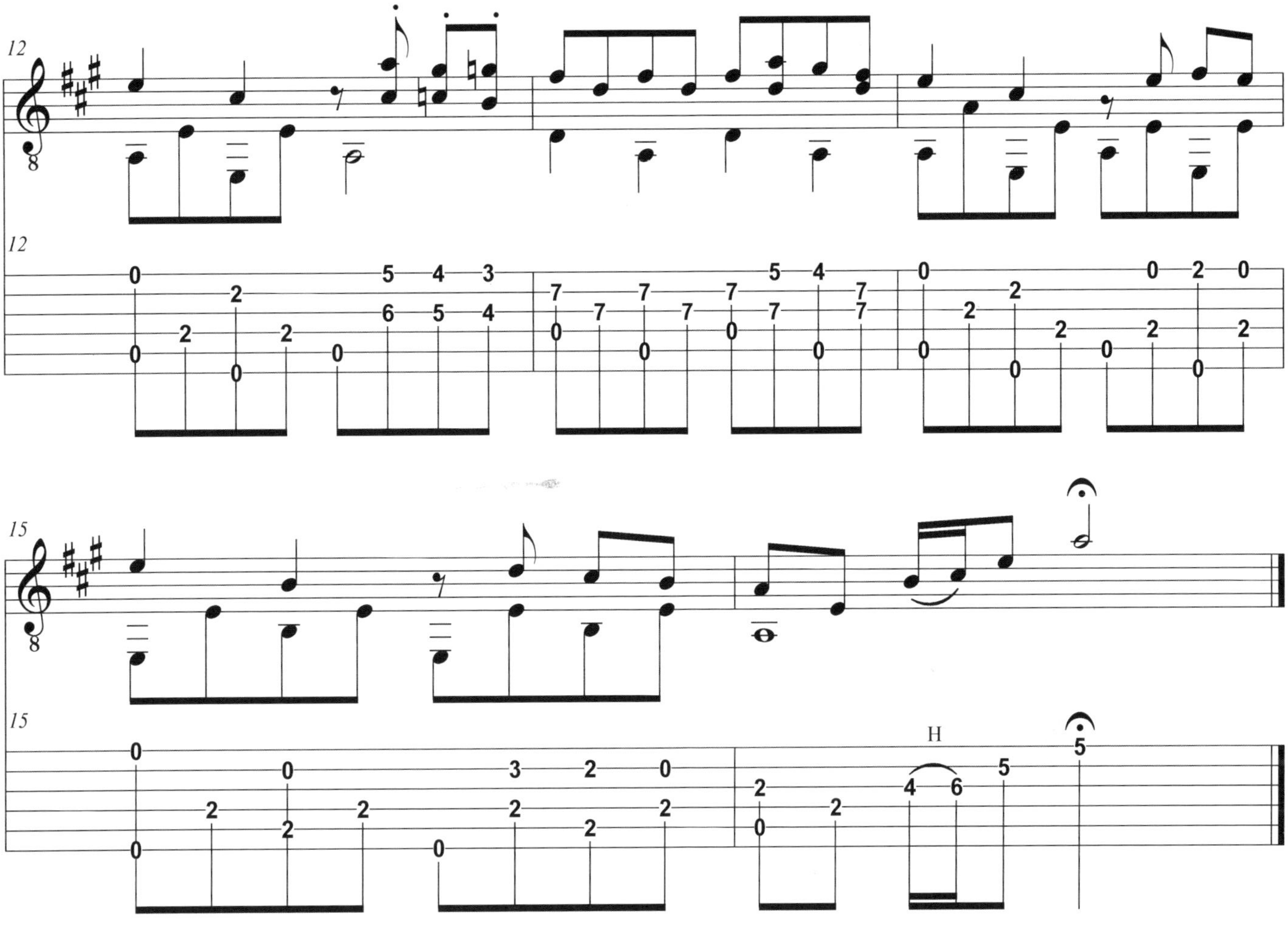
12
12
15
15
H

Roll in My Sweet Baby's Arms

11

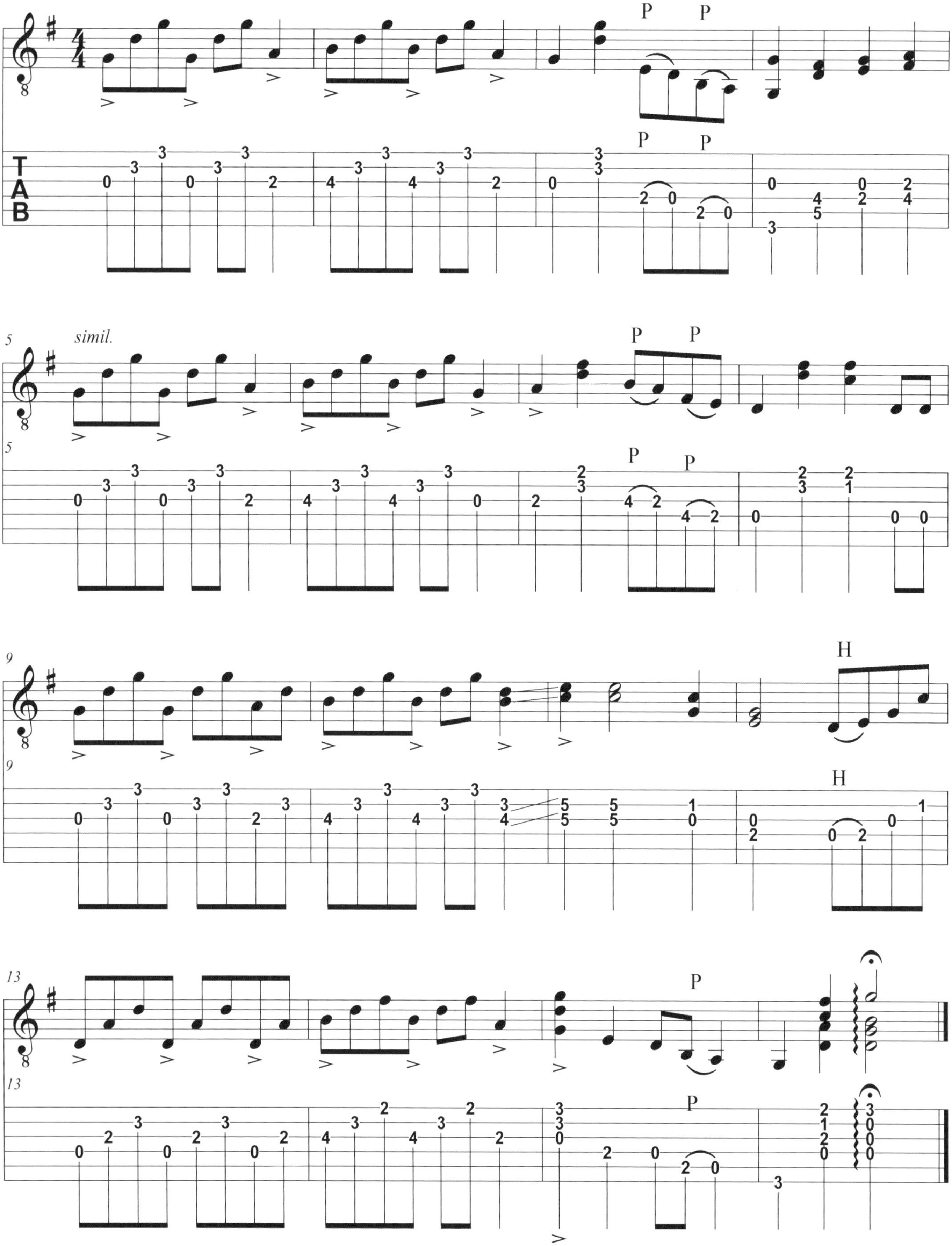

The Crawdad Song

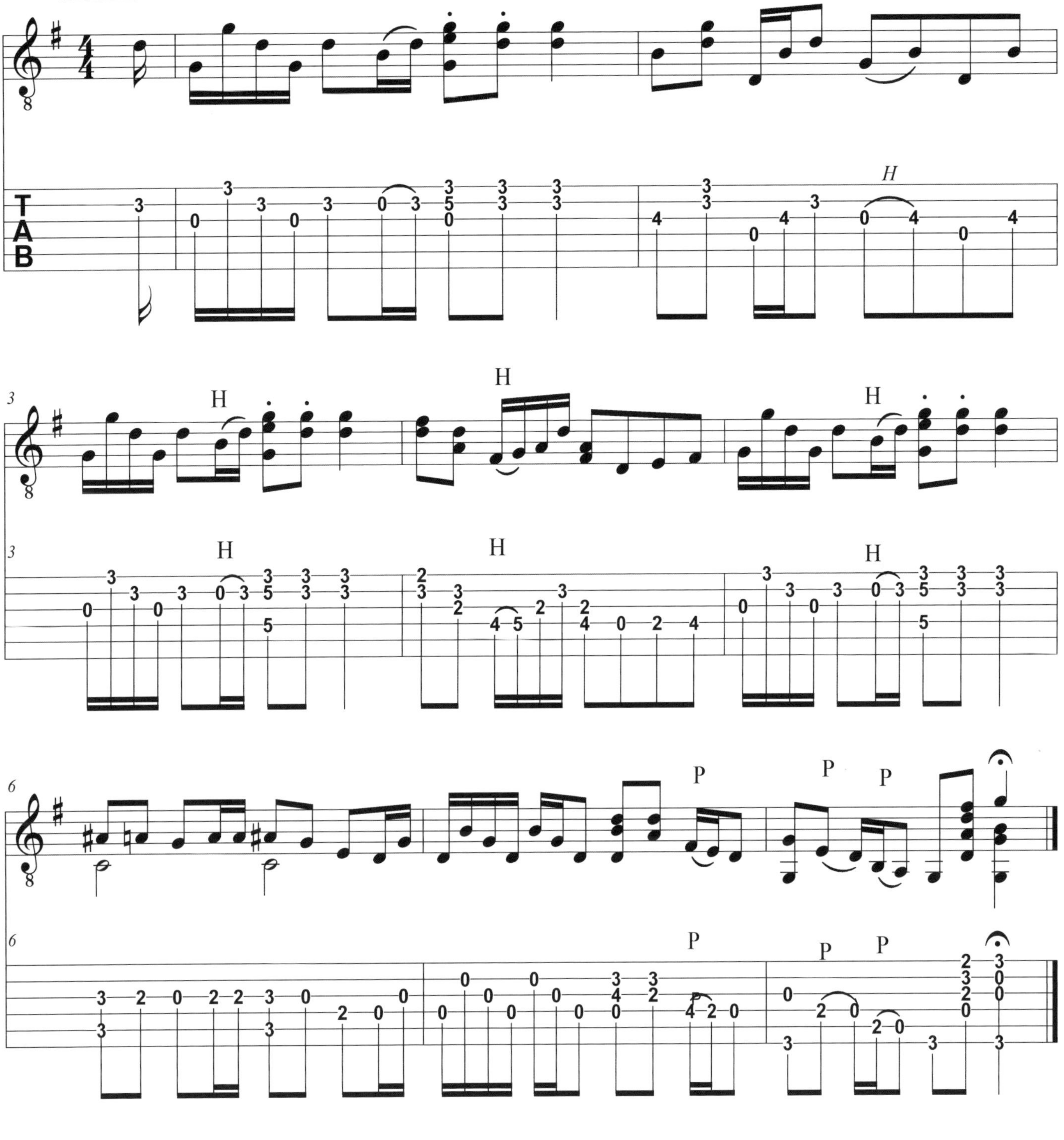

Sweet By and By

13

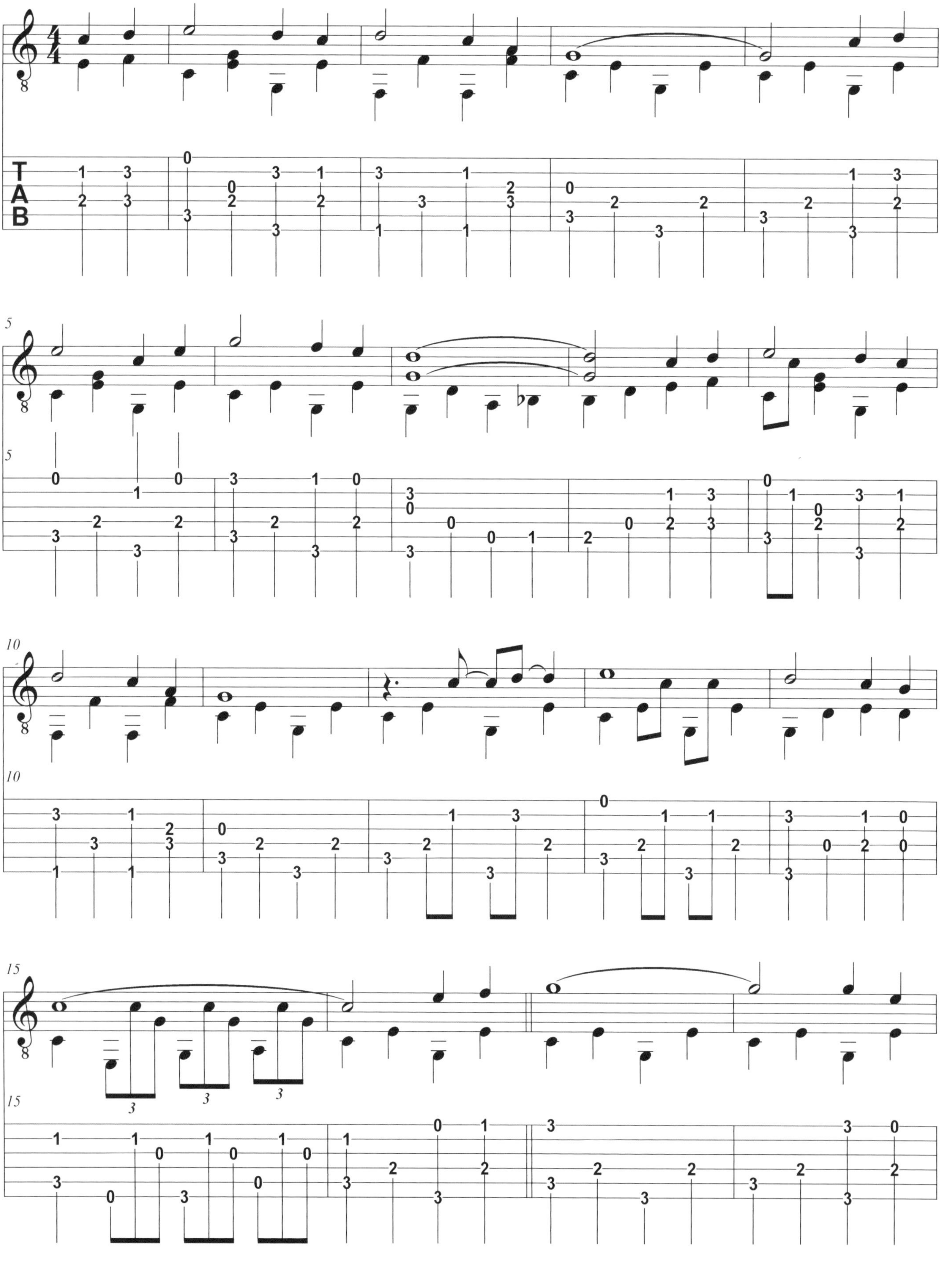

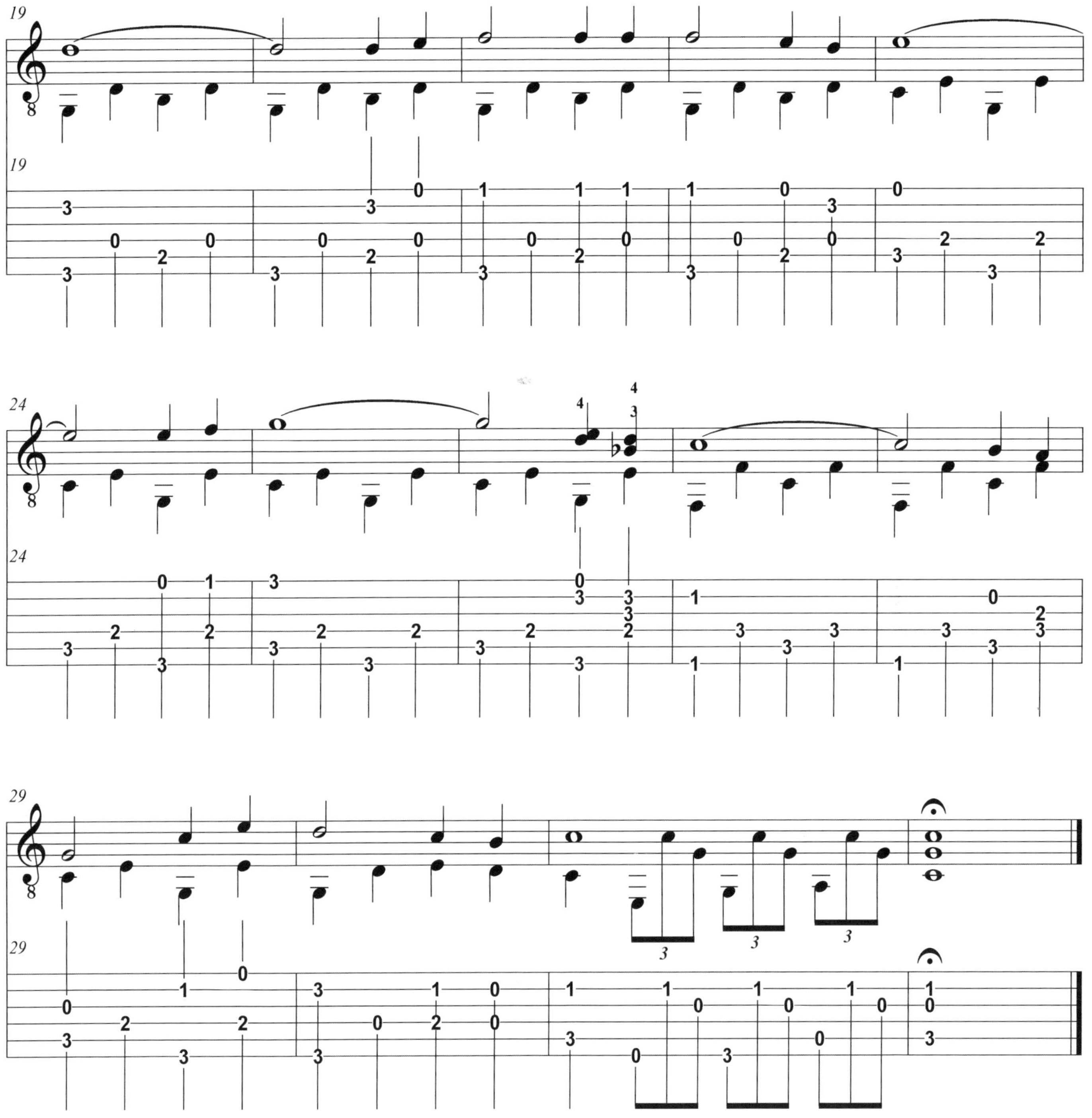

The Old Rugged Cross

14

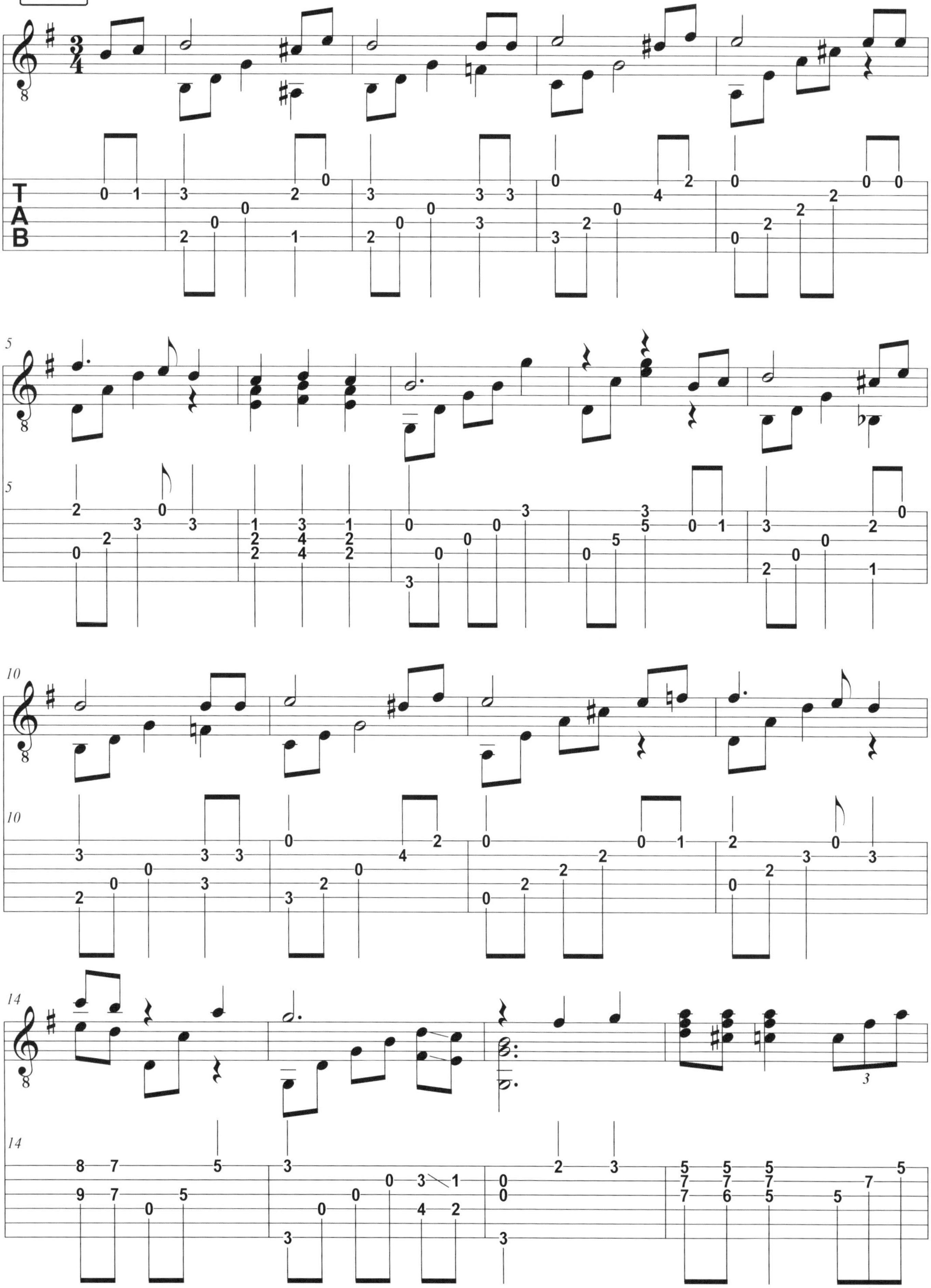

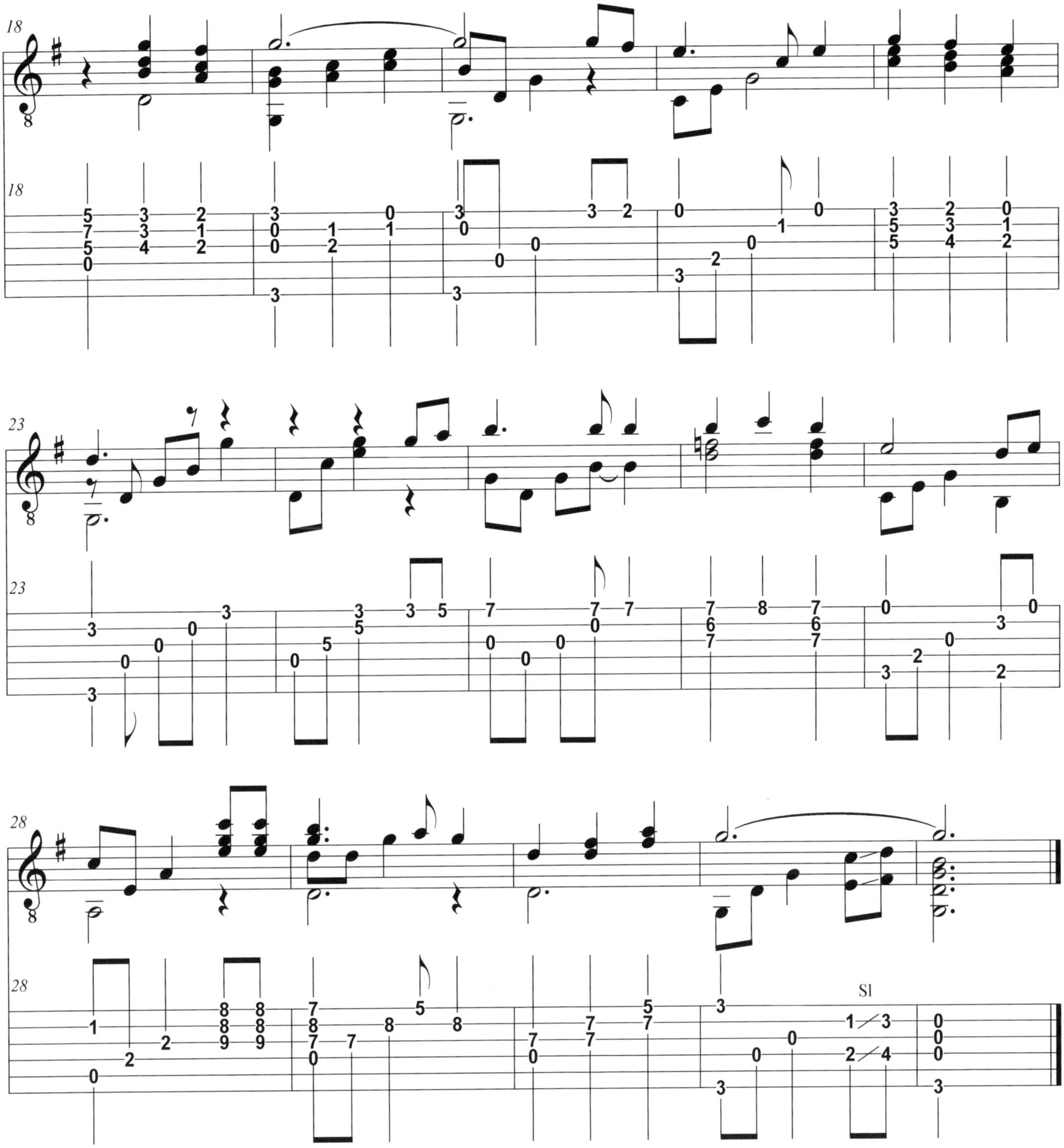
Sl

Wayfarin' Stranger

15

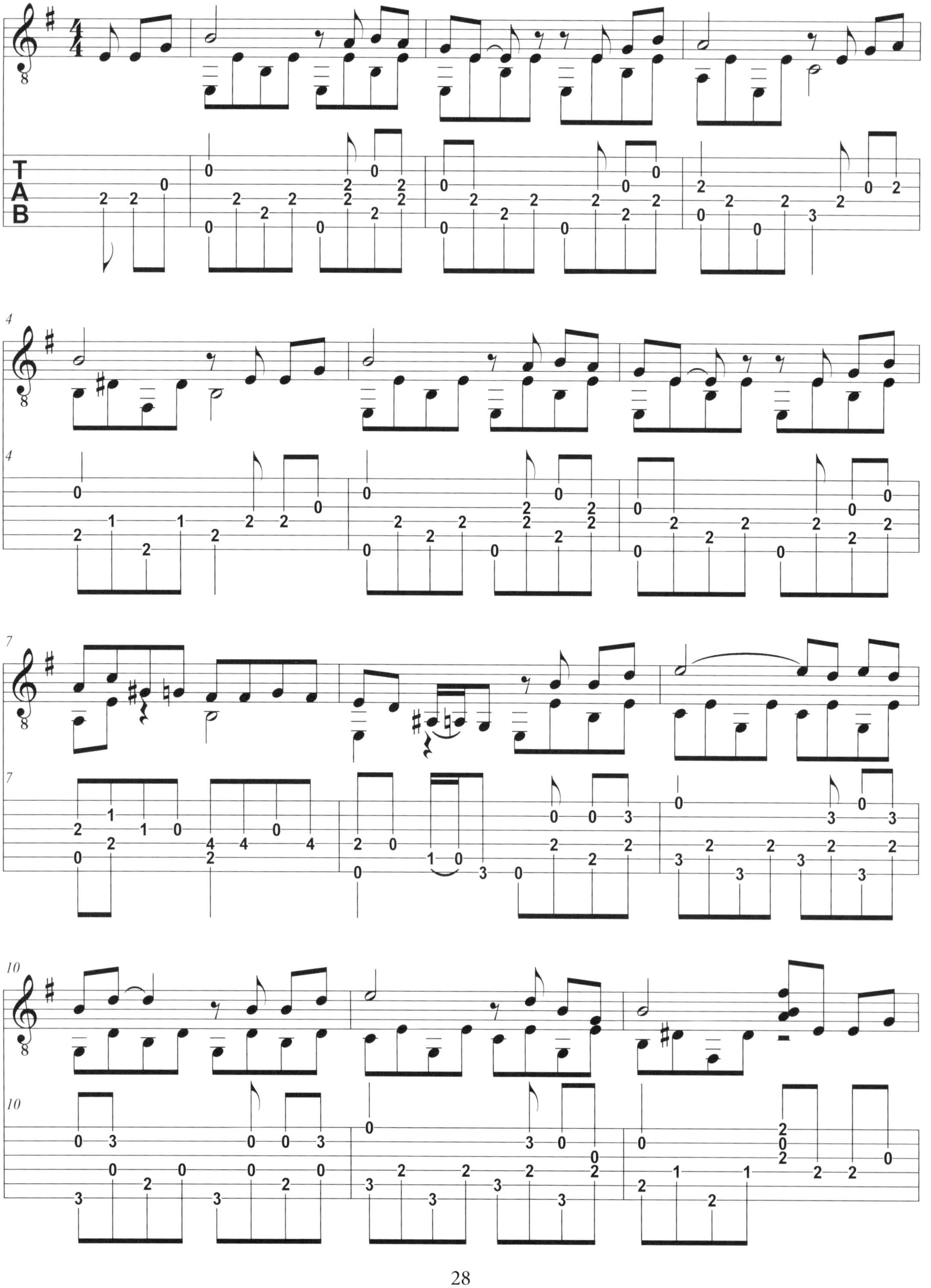

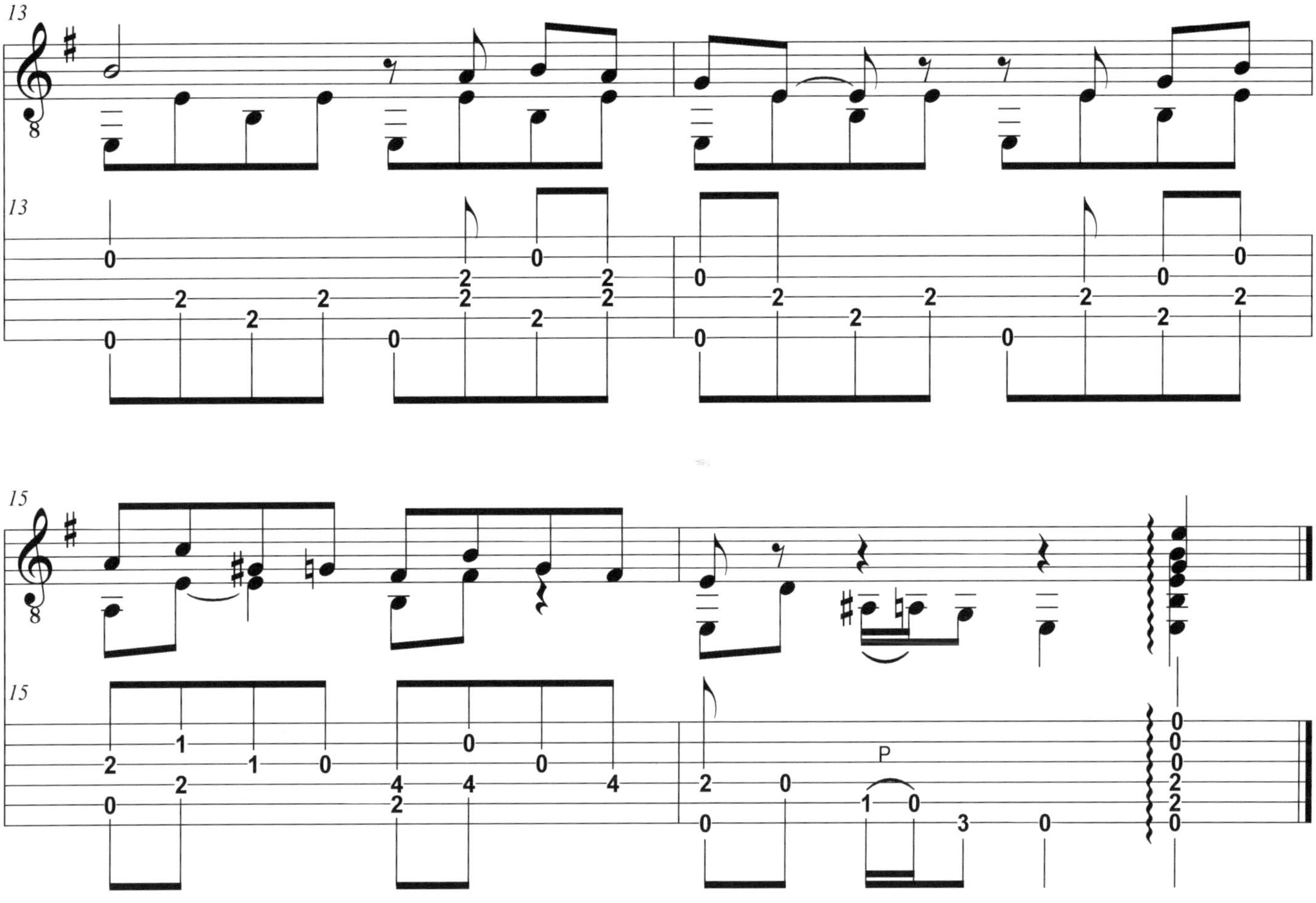

When the Roll Is Called Up Yonder

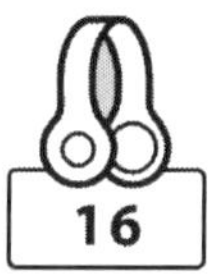

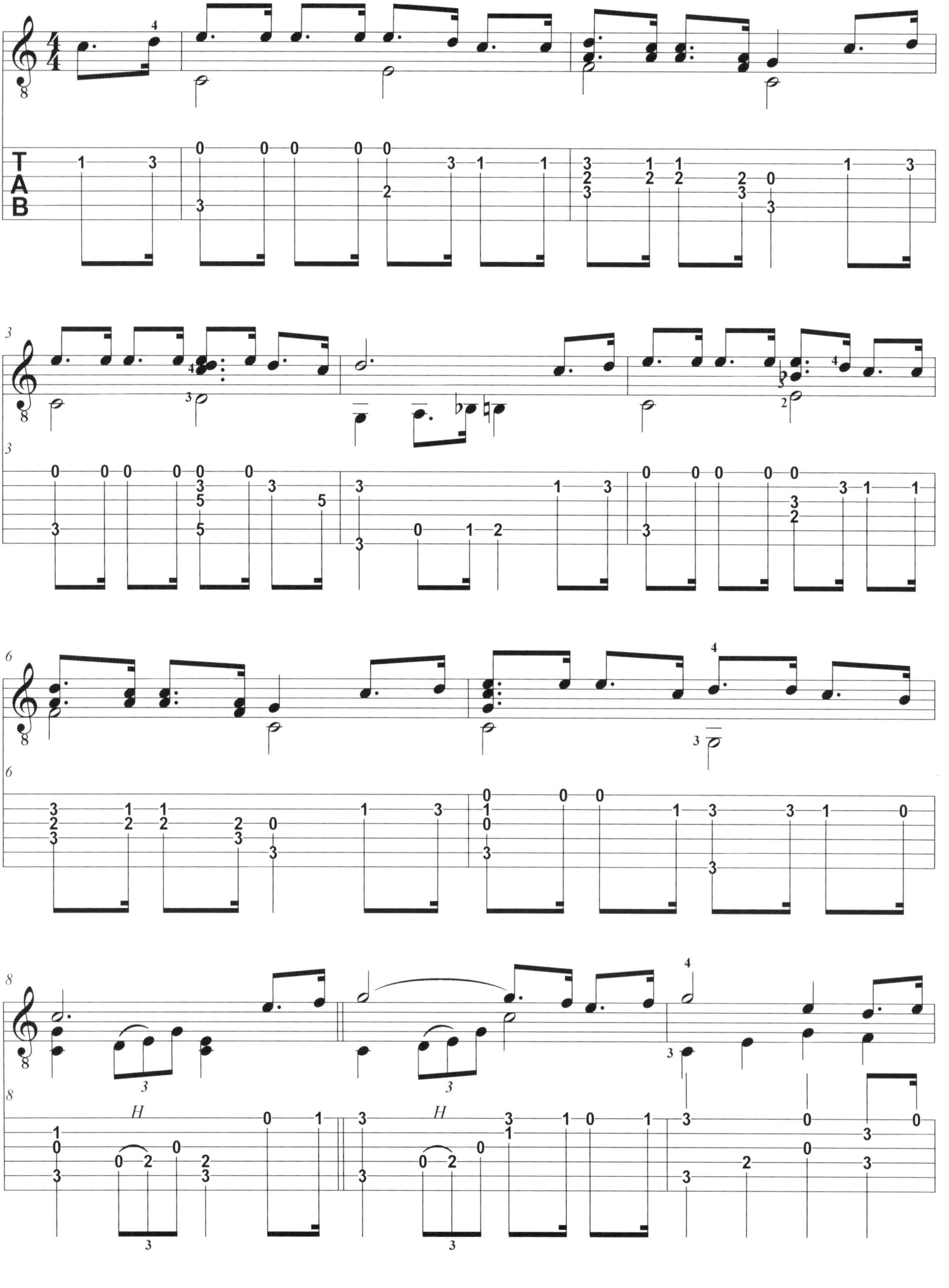

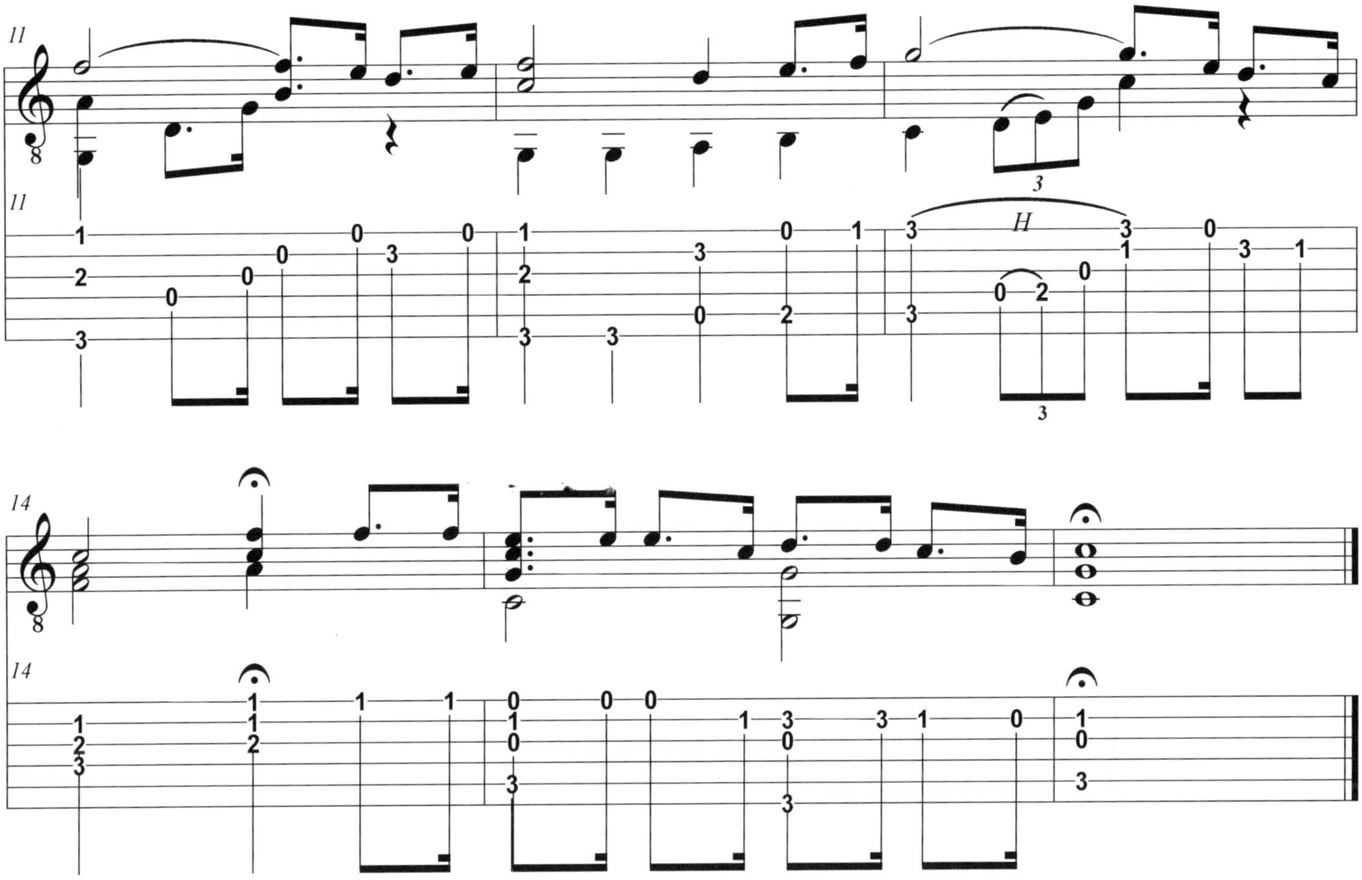

17

Just a Closer Walk with Thee

♩ = 100

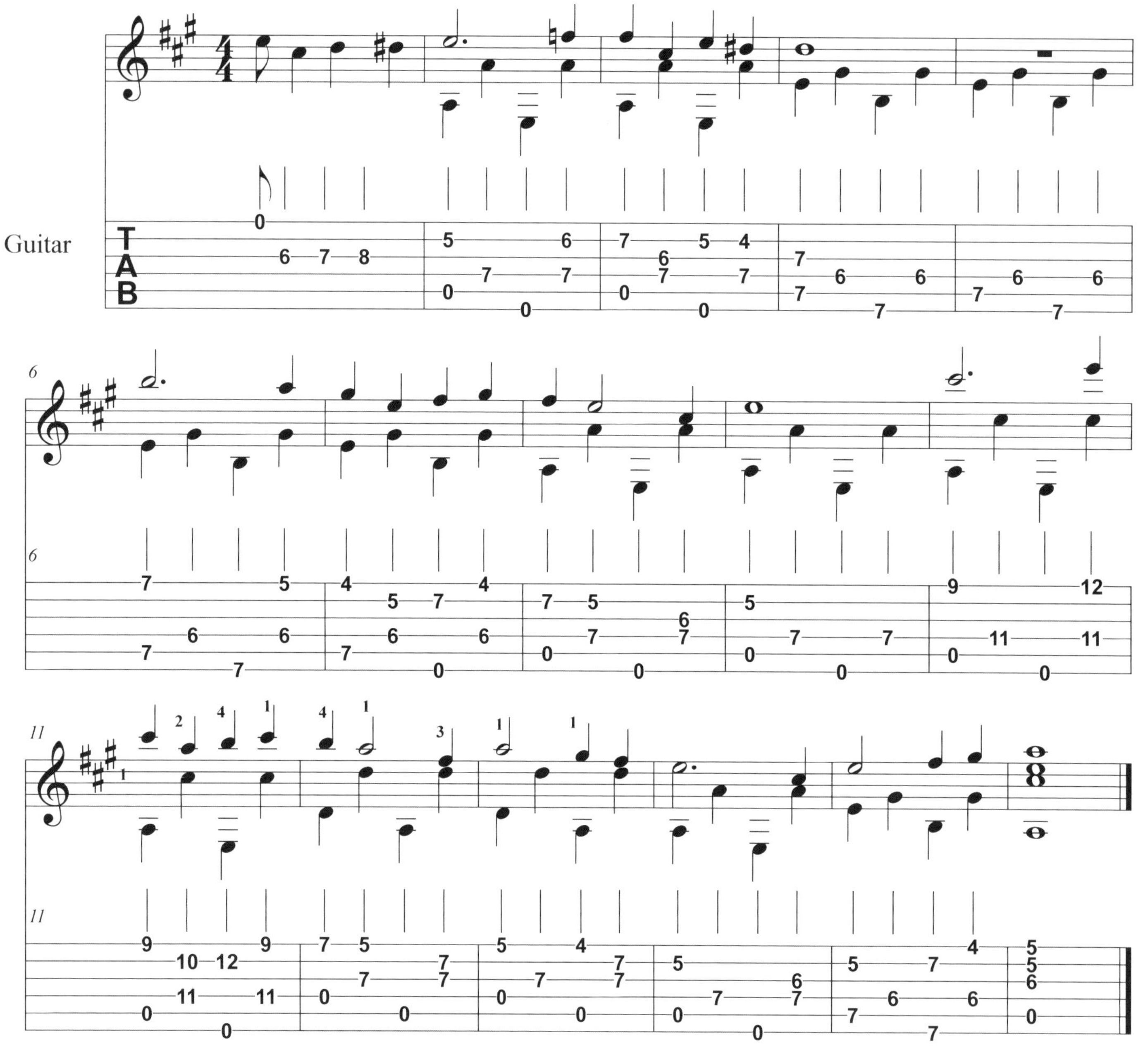

18

Just as I Am

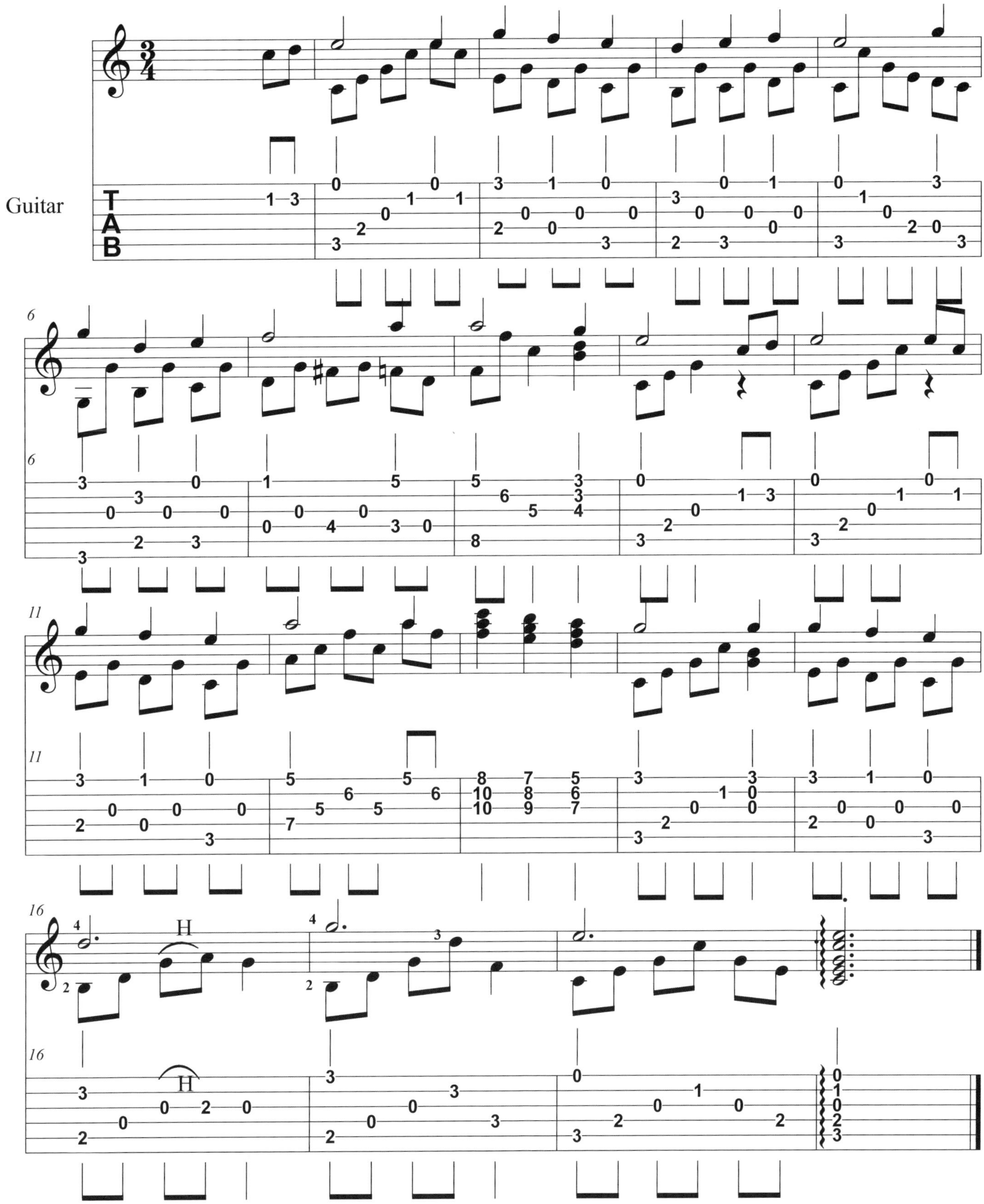

19

Wildwood Flower

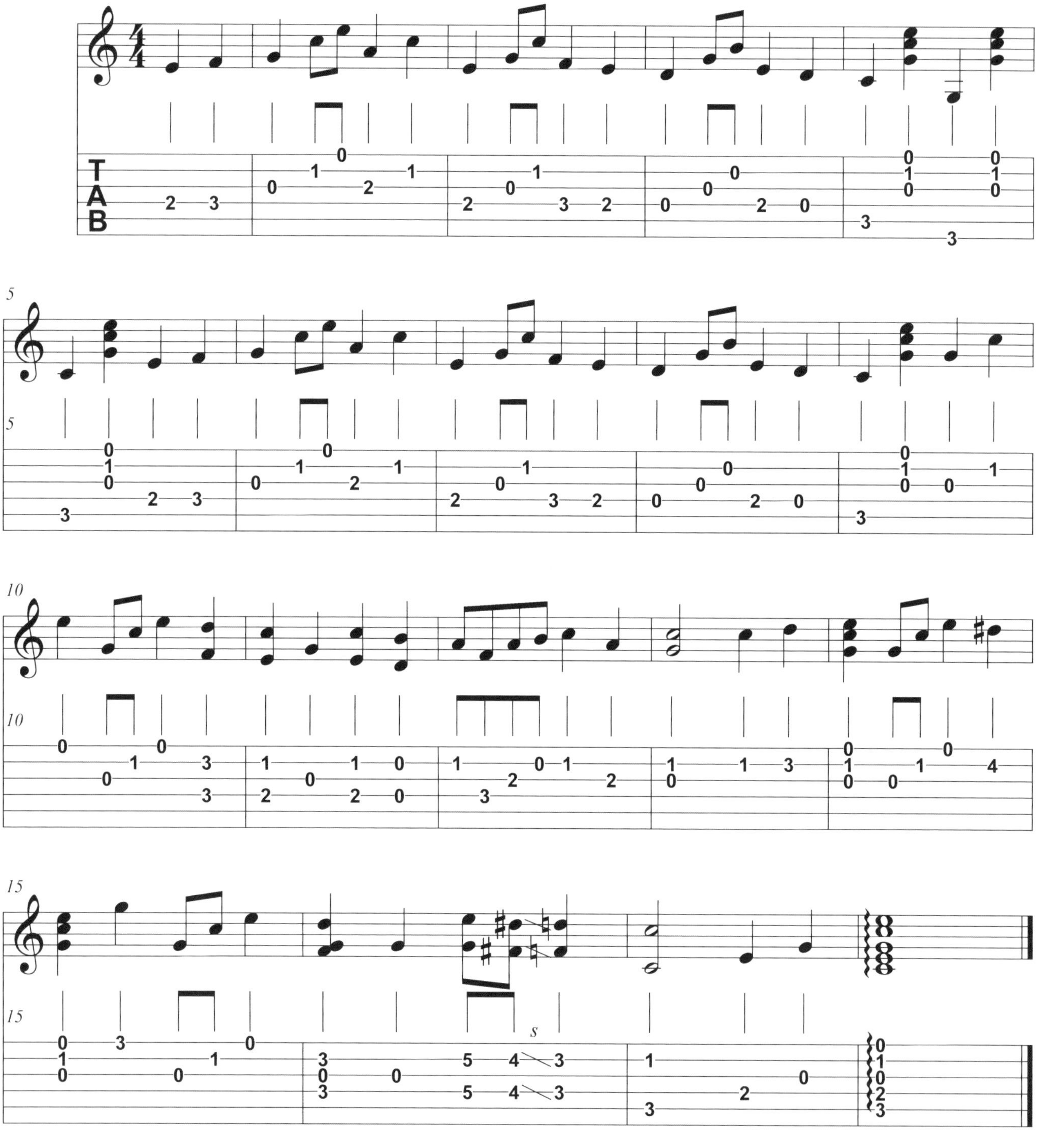

Other Mel Bay Fingerstyle Guitar Books

5-String Banjo Styles for 6-String Guitar (Dobbins)
Best of Country Guitar Solos (Flint)
Chet Atkins in Three Dimensions Vol. 1 (McClellan/Bratic)
Chet Atkins in Three Dimensions Vol. 2 (McClellan/Bratic)
Chet Atkins Off the Record (Flint)
Chet Atkins Plays Back Home Hymns (Ozee)
Complete Chet Atkins Guitar Method (Atkins/Flint)
Complete Johnny Hiland Licks & Tricks (Hiland)
Country Ballads for Fingerstyle Guitar (Flint)
Country Guitar (Flint)
Fun and Easy Fingerpicking Guitar Solos (O'Dorn)
Just Us (Buster Jones/Redmond)
Mel Bay Guitar University Fingerstyle Curriculum: Best Thumbpicking Solos (Multiple Authors)
Merle Travis Guitar Style (Flint)
24 Pieces for Guitar by Gilbert Isbin
50 Easy Contemporary Pieces for Fingerstyle Guitar (Isbin)
A Dozen Italian Diversions for Guitar Solo (DeBenedetti)
Brad Richter Solo Guitar Collection
Dixieland Tunes for Fingerstyle Guitar (Flint)
Early Jazz for Fingerstyle Guitar (Johansson)
Emmanuel Labor DVD (Tommy Emmanuel)
Fingerstyle Guitar Arranging, Composition & Performance (Gonzalez)
Fingerstyle Guitar Collection (Austen)
Fingerstyle Gig Book (Piburn)
Frailing the Guitar (Baughman)
French Tangos for Guitar (Halen)
Guitar Journals: Fingerstyle (Multiple Authors)
Master Anthology of Fingerstyle Solos Vol. 1 (Multiple Authors)
Master Anthology of Fingerstyle Solos Vol. 2 (Multiple Authors)
Master Anthology of Fingerstyle Solos Vol. 3 (Multiple Authors)
Mel Bay Guitar University Fingerstyle Curriculum: Best Contemporary Solos (Multiple Authors)
Mel Bay Guitar University Fingerstyle Curriculum: Best Ragtime Solos (Multiple Authors)
New Orleans Jazz for Fingerstyle Guitar (Hancoff)
Popular Guitar Styles: Latin & Salsa (Wolters)

Other Mel Bay Fingerstyle Guitar Books

Popular Guitar Styles: Reggae & Music of the Islands (Wolters)

Popular Guitar Styles: Samba & Bossa Nova (Wolters)

Rags, Minstrel Show Tunes & Novelty Instrumentals of Rev. Gary Davis

The Stephen Bennett Fingerstyle Collection

Tommy Emmanuel/Frank Vignola: Just Between Frets

Tommy Emmanuel/Endless Road

Tommy Emmanuel/Only

Tommy Emmanuel/The Mystery

Total Giltrap (Gordon Giltrap)

101 Easy Fingerstyle Guitar Solos (McCabe)

American Fiddle Tunes for Acoustic Guitar (Matteson)

American Treasures (Lester/Piburn)

An American Christmas (M. Lord)

Ashokan Farewell Fingerstyle Guitar Solo (Jay Ungar/Lehmann-Haupt)

Ballads and Songs of the Civil War for Guitar (Silverman)

British Fingerpicking Guitar (Grossman)

Christmas Encyclopedia: Fingerstyle Edition (Eckels)

Christmas Songs for Fingerstyle Guitar (Flint)

Easiest Fingerpicking Guitar Solos (W. Bay/Flint)

Easiest Fingerpicking Guitar for Children (McCabe)

Fingerpicking Guitar Tune Book (Flint)

Fingerstyle Guitar Tunes-Beautiful American Airs and Ballads (Gonzalez)

Fingerstyle Guitar Tunes-Beautiful Airs and Ballads of the British Isles (Gonzalez)

Fingerstyle Guitar Tunes-Christmas in the British Isles (Gonzalez)

Folk songs and Dances of the Jewish People for Acoustic Guitar (Back)

Folk Songs from the Appalachian Mountains for Acoustic Guitar (Matteson)

Global Adventures for Fingerstyle Guitarists (Eckels)

Guitar Music of Cuba (Barreiro)

Guitar Tabsongs: Bluegrass (Silverman)

Mel Bay Guitar University Fingerstyle Curriculum: Best Traditional Folk Solos (Multiple Authors)

Neshamah: Traditional Jewish Melodies (Sparks)

Sacred Music for Solo Guitar (Foster)

The Salutation: Carols from England, Scotland & Ireland (Duck Baker)